BIG IMPACT

INSIGHTS & STORIES FROM AMERICA'S NON-PROFIT LEADERS

21 Social Sector Leaders Share Master
Strategies for Shaping Change

VIVIEN HOEXTER AND LINDA C. HARTLEY

Printed in the United States of America

First Printing, 2017

Print ISBN: 978-1-54391-266-1

H2Growth Strategies LLC
325 East 77th Street
New York, NY 10075
www.h2growth.com

For our husbands, Mark and Bruce, whose love
and superb cooking gave us strength

For our parents, Corinne, Rolf, Edith and Richard, whose
emotional and financial support gave us courage

For our friend Barbara, whose belief in our
work helped make the book a reality

CONTENTS

INTRODUCTION

Leaders fascinate us.

We want to adore them, emulate them and learn from them. In the United States, corporate leaders particularly enthrall us. Visit any bookstore—retail or online—and you will find scores of books about becoming the next Steve Jobs or Sheryl Sandberg. We want to believe their advice can help us achieve the American dream of success and prosperity, through hard work, ingenuity, and regardless of gender, race, religion or the socioeconomic circumstances of birth.

Leaders in the U.S. nonprofit sector are committed to improving the quality of life on this planet, to making available more widely the possibility of achieving the American dream, undergirded by the values of a democratic society: liberty, equality and justice. And while the definition of the American dream will continue to evolve as it is compared to reality, it serves as a beacon for those who seek to create a "more just, verdant and peaceful world."[1]

Inspired by the wise, compassionate and innovative leaders we have met during decades working in and with nonprofit organizations, we set out to write a book about nonprofit leadership. Between October 2016 and June 2017, we conducted a series of interviews with nearly 50 leaders of the U.S. nonprofit sector. These are CEOs of major private foundations, large nonprofit organizations, associations of nonprofits and a media outlet serving the nonprofit sector. Those interviewed represent foundations such as the Annie E. Casey, Ford, Ms. Foundation for Women, Newman's Own, Robin Hood, Rockefeller Brothers Fund, San Francisco Community, William and Flora Hewlett, as well as organizations such as Bank Street College, Bard College, the Brady Campaign to Prevent Gun Violence, Convergence Network, DoSomething.org, Freedom to Marry, Humentum, Nature Conservancy, New York City Opera, PBS, the Silicon Valley Education Foundation and uAspire.[2]

What we gleaned from these interviews was inspiring, enlightening and empowering. Leader after leader shared key lessons they have distilled from their long experience tackling societal, professional and personal challenges.

What we found was that many of these leaders are effecting positive social change, often without a lot of fanfare or publicity. We decided to pay tribute to what they

---

1   The John D. and Catherine T. MacArthur Foundation supports creative people, effective institutions and influential networks building a more just, verdant, and peaceful world. https://www.macfound.org/about/.
2   For a complete list of interviewees, see Appendix 1.

have learned in their lives and careers and how they and their organizations are making change. Our hope is that this information will be useful to you, the reader, as you strive to make positive changes in your own organizations and communities.

As experts in the global nonprofit and fund-raising community, we help organizations build on their strengths and improve their results. We partner with nonprofits and with businesses working with nonprofits and start-ups that, like nonprofits, need access to funding. For us, hearing the personal, and often profoundly moving, reflections of the nearly 50 leaders we interviewed was affirming and powerful.

In Chapters 1, 5, 9, 13, 17, 21 and 25, we share the lessons we learned. In the other chapters, we include highlights from some of the interviews that best illustrate these lessons, and in the last chapter, we suggest additional reading and exercises for those who wish to explore the subject more closely. We do this so you too can learn, laugh and be moved by the hard-won insights and experiences of the people who run the foundations and nonprofits that change our world daily.

This book is our thank you to these men and women who contribute so much to the quality of life in our country and around the world.

Vivien Hoexter and Linda C. Hartley
New York, NY
August 30, 2017

CHAPTER 1

Sharpen Your Leadership Skills

There is no one recipe for successful social change. The issues are too disparate and the conditions in different situations too dissimilar. However, when we analyzed the interviews we had conducted, we found that successful leaders, organizations and movements tend to share certain traits, habits and skills. Anyone who wants to make positive change in their community, country or farther afield can learn from these patterns.

We identified seven of these principles, and we chose to begin with the leader, radiating outward in concentric circles to the organization, groups of organizations and finally, to the general public. Symbolically, this emphasizes the importance of starting with you, the leader, in any attempt to make positive change in the world.

In this chapter, we explore the first theme, "Sharpen Your Leadership Skills," with instructive examples from our interviewees' accounts and our personal and professional experience. The chapter is followed by highlights from three interviews that have much to say on this topic.

Learning what it means to be an effective leader is a lifelong process, and we pass on many suggestions, some of them quite unexpected, that our interviewees shared with us. We also observe these traits in some of the most inspiring leaders we have known and worked with.

A. Build Emotional Intelligence and Self-Awareness

Our leaders have emotional intelligence and self-awareness in abundance. This will come as no surprise to you. What is interesting is how candid they are about how they acquired this wisdom and how they have never ceased to refine the insights that they have gained.

Many shared the pain of transcending painfully difficult experiences, like the loss of a loved one—the death of a child or the untimely death of a parent, sibling or spouse. One such story came from Larry Kramer, President of the William and Flora Hewlett Foundation, which "advances ideas and supports institutions to promote a better world," with a particular focus on the environment.

When he was a young boy, Kramer says, his biological father left his family. His mother remarried when Larry was 8, and as a young man in his 20s, he lost this second father. Although his adopted father was not a highly communicative person, his death left a huge void. "After my dad died," he says, "I realized how relationships make your life. I could never replace the relationship I had with my father. ... This sense of the importance of relationships is something I take into my work."

Chip Edelsberg, consultant and former CEO of the Jim Joseph Foundation, lost his daughter when she was a young woman, in what he calls "a perversion of the natural cycle of life." Edelsberg is Jewish, and, he says that because his faith teaches that one should choose life, that is the path he and his wife have chosen to follow, despite their grief.

Leon Botstein, president of Bard College, also focused on the good that can come from the most harrowing of trials. He says, "By far the worst thing that ever happened to me was that I had a daughter who was killed at the age of 8. That puts all other disappointments and failures in relief. What I learned from it is that one needs to find a way to rescue victory from the jaws of defeat. Rather than turning disappointment and tragedy into an excuse for feeling like a powerless victim, I try to recognize the unintended gift that comes from tragedy and failure. It's like a prizefight: The key is having the ability to get up again after getting knocked down. The other important thing I learned is that you have to be fully aware of the tenuousness of any plan or any notion. You can't control what happens, and you're constantly at the mercy of the unexpected."

He continues, "Bad things allow you to always balance the relative values that you cherish, and to cease being dependent on what other people think of you. You have to learn to be confident in the judgment that you make of what you think is right, as opposed to the popular perception. The right things may not always be the popular things."

Perhaps because of the magnitude of the challenges they are facing, some of our leaders, already highly successful, are obsessed with continuing to grow and develop.

Henry Timms, Executive Director of 92Y, a leading cultural and community institution, says he wants to work harder at being a great leader. He acknowledges that most people would say that he has achieved a remarkable amount at a relatively young age. He admits that he could easily settle into a routine and try a little less hard.

He tells how Eric Lange, the associate human resources director at 92Y and a noted human resources expert, recommended that he should not be afraid to admit to his own fallibility. Timms says, "Because everybody—no matter how impressive you can persuade the world you actually are— everyone goes home feeling slightly broken one time or another. In all of us, there's that. He really reminded me to talk openly when I wasn't feeling confident, and when I was worried about stuff, and when things had gone wrong."

The conventional view is that leaders should never betray any sign of weakness, and that they should always project an image of strength. In the 21st century, however, great leaders have permission to be vulnerable as well as powerful. This makes them more accessible to the people they are working with, and in the last analysis, more deserving of respect.

Timms says that since he first received this advice, he has been much more open to discussing problems as they arise. And in return, he has been repaid with increased loyalty and dedication, as well as much more helpful input, from his staff, board and volunteers.

It is eye-opening insights like these that compelled us to share these stories. We believe that the experience of these leaders can provide a rich and compelling education in the leadership of modern nonprofits and foundations.

Hearing these profound stories and insights, we came to appreciate the management value of sharing personal lessons learned within organizations, to build greater cohesion, camaraderie and enhance problem-solving within teams.

Alice Hockenbury, vice president for public policy and advocacy at the Girl Scouts of America, has reflected deeply on her management style: "Listening is a skill I have worked hard to acquire," she says. "Younger staff members have made me think about outdated ways of doing work. I am trying to give them more opportunities to lead the projects. My ideas are not always the best, even though I have been in the workforce over 30 years.

"Anything to do with more online or social media, they always have better insights into how to amplify the work that we are doing in unique, new ways."

We heard similar stories over and over again, confirming that our leaders are committed to growing and adapting throughout their careers.

B. Gather a Variety of Life and Work Experiences

Many of our interviewees stress the importance of stepping out of the community where you grew up to work in other places and appreciate other cultures. They also advise those who would like ultimately to go into management to work in direct service with the people an organization is serving.

Dorothy Stoneman, founder and president of YouthBuild, has helped hundreds of thousands of disadvantaged young people graduate from high school and get well-paid jobs. She says, "Embed yourself in a completely different community long enough to make a difference. Your life will be shaped by the choices you make in your twenties." She is referring to organizations like the Peace Corps and Vista, but her advice could apply equally well to someone moving to another city or state.

One of us worked for American Field Service Intercultural Programs/USA, an organization that sends high school students to live abroad, often with families, for periods of a month to a year. Those young people come back to the United States transformed, their horizons widened and their maturity greatly increased. They almost universally acknowledge that being immersed in another culture, often without first knowing the language, has taught them empathy, humility and the power of interdependence.

Bill Ulfelder, New York executive director of the Nature Conservancy, emphasizes how he preaches the benefits of learning new languages to young people. "Go see other cultures, travel the country, leave the country, have those experiences." He himself spent time during his college years studying conservation in the Peruvian Amazon. From then on, he was committed to global conservation.

Regardless of your background, you can succeed in the nonprofit world. Some of our interviewees recommend working in the public or private sectors before entering the nonprofit sector. Others think young people should pursue what they want to do right from the start.

Our own experience is that it doesn't matter. One of us began her career in the corporate world; the other has always worked in the nonprofit sector. We believe there are pros and cons to both trajectories. We agree that passion for a mission is important. We also think developing functional expertise is critical.

It may be more difficult to gain the necessary experience in information technology, human resources or finance in the nonprofit sector, since so many nonprofits are small and cannot afford to train their staff members in the way large corporations do. In the program and fund-raising areas, which are a quintessential part of the nonprofit world, it is more possible to develop the expertise while on the job.

Kevin McMahon is CEO of the Pittsburgh Cultural Trust, whose mission is the cultural and economic revitalization of a 14-block arts and entertainment/residential neighborhood in downtown Pittsburgh. He says, "It's critically important to at least attempt to pick and direct your career by getting involved in high-quality institutions, places that are large enough to learn from but not so large that you get pigeonholed into one narrow field too early."

C. Seek Out Mentors

All our leaders emphasize the importance of seeking out mentors at every stage of their lives and careers. Some can identify mentors from their middle and high school years. Others talk about mentors they had in college, graduate school or when they were starting out.

Brian Gallagher, CEO of United Way Worldwide, grew up in a family that often did not have enough to eat. He describes a basketball coach whose son he became friends with. The son had another friend whose mother was like a mother to Gallagher. Without these other families, he would never have considered that he could go to college. And without the model of the social workers who helped him and his family, he might not have pursued a degree in social work, which determined his future career.

Dan Cardinali is CEO of Independent Sector, the "only national membership organization that brings together a diverse set of nonprofits, foundations and corporations to advance the common good."[3] "Early on in my career," he says, "I was very, very lucky to have a whole series of mentors, most of whom were Jesuit priests and brothers. I really learned the core sets of principles that guide my life professionally from that Jesuit training. At the heart of that is this notion of putting the individual person as an end in and of him or herself, and not as a means to an end. Human and community flourishing are the primary goals of all activity and all work."

---

3   Independent Sector, "About". https://www.independentsector.org/about/ (accessed August 7, 2017).

Amy Houston is managing director for management assistance and administration at the Robin Hood Foundation, whose goal is to end poverty in New York City. Karl Andros, she says, was one of the first executive directors she worked for, and is still a good friend and mentor. Originally a musician, who began playing weekday gigs in public schools, he discovered that the performing arts could engage students—and ultimately discovered how the arts can be a powerful way to teach reading and writing. "He is most inspiring to me," Houston says, "because he is never resting. He is constantly asking questions and constantly looking for new and better ways to work. And, most importantly, he inspires that in everyone around him."

Aria Finger is CEO of DoSomething.org, "a global movement for good," which empowers 5.5 million young people to make positive change, both online and off. It runs campaigns for young people such as clothing youth in homeless shelters and "tweeting your governor to create a cleaner, safer, better America."

Finger celebrates the help she received from the founder of DoSomething.org, Nancy Lublin, for whom she worked for 10 years before becoming CEO. "She is one of those people who lifts up everyone," Finger says. I was 25 or 26, and she took me out for a hot chocolate and said, "You're going to be the next CEO of DoSomething. I'm grooming you to be the next CEO." I didn't believe her. I don't even remember if I said no, but I thought no. But she was true to her word. She has given me so much and the only reason I'm successful today is because of her."

CHAPTER 2

Shael Polakow-Suransky

President, Bank Street College of Education

Shael Polakow-Suransky became the eighth president of Bank Street College of Education in 2014. Under his leadership, Bank Street is building new models for teacher education, expanding its work with public schools and child care centers, and developing an applied research center focused on early childhood policy and practice.

Previously, Polakow-Suransky was the second-in-command at the New York City Department of Education, the nation's largest school system, serving as chief academic officer and senior deputy chancellor. Overseeing teaching and learning across more than 1,600 district schools, he was a strong advocate for teacher and principal autonomy, balanced accountability and reforms designed to improve learning experiences for the city's most vulnerable students.

Earlier in his career, he worked as a teacher and founding principal of Bronx International High School. He holds a B.A. from Brown University, where Ted Sizer was his mentor, and a master's in educational leadership from Bank Street. He is the first alumnus to serve as Bank Street's president.

Bank Street College of Education

Bank Street College of Education is a leader in early childhood education, a pioneer in improving the quality of classroom practice and a national advocate for children and their families. Since 1916, it has been at the forefront of understanding how children learn and grow. From early childhood centers and schools to hospitals and museums, Bank Street has built a national reputation on the simple fact that its graduates know how to do the work that is right for children.

Through its Graduate School of Education, Children's Programs, Division of Innovation, Policy and Research, and Bank Street Education Center, the college helps transform the way teachers and children engage in learning. Learning becomes an active, lifelong endeavor in which children and adults alike engage as careful observers, experimenters and creative thinkers. The approach recognizes that children do not all learn at the same rate or in the same way. Effective teaching and learning demand a range of strategies to meet multiple needs.

At the graduate school, educators are trained in a model that combines the study of human development, learning theory and sustained clinical practice to ensure significant development as a teacher or leader prior to graduation. The School for Children, Family Center, Head Start and Liberty LEADS foster children's development by providing diverse opportunities for social, emotional, cognitive and physical growth. In addition, the school further supports positive outcomes for children, educators and families through professional development programs, research projects and other key initiatives at the district, state and federal levels.

Shael Polakow-Suransky

Who has had the greatest influence on you as a professional?

I started as a teacher here in New York City. When I was in my fourth year of teaching, I came to Bank Street to do my master's in educational leadership and was assigned to an internship with Eric Nadelstern, the principal of International High School in Queens. The school, which he had designed in the 1980s, was for recent immigrants. At the time, it was one of the most successful models in the city for that population.

I ended up first interning under Nadelstern and then working together with him to found a version of that school in the Bronx, where I became principal. Ultimately, when Joel Klein became chancellor of the New York City Department of Education, he hired both of us to work on the effort to create new schools. As a leader, Nadelstern is someone who believes deeply in autonomy as one of the most important preconditions for success. Working under him, I had a tremendous amount of flexibility and freedom to figure out how to get from point A to point B. I also had a lot of clarity around what was meant by point B.

That sort of philosophy is unusual in public education and in government in general. Public education systems more typically regulate the inputs, trying to control how you do each step with the hope that that will lead to quality outcomes. His idea was that if you're really clear on the outcomes, it is less critical how you get there. If you give talented, entrepreneurial leaders the freedom to figure out the process, you are more likely to attract and retain them.

That definitely had a big impact both on my own development as a leader and also on the work that we did at the Department of Education for many years. That work involved restructuring the whole bureaucracy around some of these principles, and bringing in the kinds of leaders at different levels of the organization who could rethink how schools are organized.

During the Bloomberg era, we ended up opening roughly 800 new schools. It was the largest effort like that that's ever happened in this country. The graduation rates during the time prior to that administration had been consistently 50 percent. It was almost as if the system was designed every year to produce 50 percent of the kids not graduating. Under Mayor Michael Bloomberg, that started to shift rapidly. By the time he left office, the graduation rate was close to 70 percent, and the dropout rate was cut in half, from roughly 20 percent to 10 percent. There was a really deep transformation that occurred, and a lot of it had to do with Nadelstern's core idea about autonomy.

You can't regulate your way to success. You have to allow the people who are implementing the work—who are really close to the ground—a lot of flexibility. You have to put as much decision-making as close as possible to the people who have to implement it. And that means you have to build the system to attract a certain kind of leader. Expecting middle managers to follow a checklist has never worked to improve or run schools. If that's the thing that the school system is asking people to do, that's the kind of leaders you're going to get. If you're asking people to reinvent school—to figure out how to change learning outcomes for kids—you have to give them the flexibility to do it, and that attracts much stronger leaders.

Thus far, what have been the worst and best events in your life, and what did those experiences teach you?

I was married before my current marriage, and my wife died of cancer. She was in her 30s when she died. She had already had a bout of cancer. It had gone into remission and then it came back. She only survived three years after it came back.

It's always hard when you lose someone that you love. But to have someone who is that young die is unusual. It taught me a lot about how important it is to really use your life. You don't have any guarantees about how long you will live. Making compromises that put off things that you care deeply about, or not addressing deep issues that need to be dealt with, is really easy to do. That experience made me realize how much each choice you make matters. It's very possible to lose your health and, with it, to lose a lot of freedom and to miss out on a lot of the things that you imagined you would always be able to do.

On the positive side, the process of starting a new school is an incredibly creative process. It takes creativity to build an organization from the ground up that didn't exist before, to shape its details intimately, to choose the people who are going to work there, and to build a culture both for the adults and the children. I really enjoyed that work. It was very challenging work, incredibly demanding in both intellectual and emotional ways.

I was young—I was 29 when I designed the school—so I was really new to a leadership role and new to every step of building an organization. But I really believe that public institutions have the potential to be transformative in people's lives. The opportunity to create a school centered around the needs of immigrant students and their families was a privilege. In order to get into our school, students had to fail the English language assessment and be new to the country.

We had over 40 languages spoken in the school. In addition, many of our students were refugees from war-torn areas. It was a very cosmopolitan group of kids, and they had been through a lot. It was exciting to create an environment that was really successful for them.

We were working out of Morris High School, one of the oldest school buildings in the Bronx. It had regularly been the worst school in the city for many years. They were enrolling about 700 students each year as ninth-graders and graduating about 70 each year from the 12th grade.

The model to transform Morris was to create several small schools in the same building as the larger school. Each small school started with just a ninth grade and then phased up year by year until they had all four grades. At the same time, the large existing school stopped accepting students and phased out as each of the remaining grades graduated. After four years, there were four successful small schools in place of the large school that was failing. My school was one of those four.

The year before we started, I interviewed the assistant principal who was in charge of hiring to understand what it was like working in this community. He was about two weeks away from school opening and had 30 vacancies on a staff of roughly 200. He said to me, "At this point, if you walk through my door and you've got a pulse, you're going to get a job, because I can't fill these spots. And the main problem is we're in a two-fare zone (which means that you have to take a subway and a bus to get here), and so people don't want to deal with that. And there's not much parking."

Six months later, we started hiring for an additional group of six teachers, in the same building in the same neighborhood. We got 500 applicants for six spots. As we went through the applicant pool, what became clear to me was that it's not at all hard to attract talented teachers to a tough neighborhood in a two-fare zone if they believe the thing they're coming to do is going to make a difference. People will work really hard and go far out of their way if they feel like they can have an impact. It was as simple as coming up with a good plan that was compelling and exciting. It was as simple as starting to tell the story of what this place could be.

The school is still there. And it's thriving. After four years, the schools on that campus had a combined graduation rate of roughly 70 percent. That was more than triple what it had been, and it has stayed strong. It's still one of the poorest neighborhoods in the city, and there are still a lot of challenges, but the schools on this campus are rich, vibrant places with lots of very engaging work for children and a responsiveness to their social and emotional needs.

The kids are really known well. The school makes it central to its mission to understand who the students are, what they need, and how to nurture them. When you do that, you develop a lot of trust. The old Morris High School, before we went through this restructuring, had 50 adults with at least part of their job descriptions related to security.

Once we finished the restructuring, that number was down to 12. The level of incidents of disciplinary infractions had dropped significantly. This was because instead of building up a security apparatus to control the kids, we built good relationships that actually made students feel like they could talk to adults when there was a problem. For example, one day I had a young man from Serbia come in and tell me that there was going to be a fight after school. He had brought a knife and had hidden it on the roof of the bus stop outside of the school. This was a kid who had been in several fights already. He was not easy, but we had spent a lot of time together because of those incidents, and he had grown to trust me.

We made agreements about how to avoid fighting, and one of them was that he could come to me if something was going to happen, and I would help him. That's what you want, and it's not that complicated. You want to get to a point with kids, even if they are prone to violence or have other kinds of challenges, where they don't have to deal with it by themselves—because they're not always going to make good decisions. And in fact, when you look at some of the problems that exist across urban education, a lot of it comes down to the fact that the structures that exist in schools prevent adults from building trusting relationships with kids.

What, if anything, keeps you up at night?

Let me first provide a little context on the work I do now running Bank Street College of Education. We run a Graduate School of Education that prepares roughly 700 teachers and school leaders each year. We also have a school for children starting at 6 months old and going through eighth grade. It is a lab school, but also a sought-after private, independent school in New York City. We have a policy arm that works with states and school districts to think about ways to change some of the systemic levers that prevent schools from succeeding. Finally, we have a professional development arm that is in the trenches working in schools here in New York City and across the country, mostly in urban districts, to build capacity.

Those four aspects of the organization all have different needs, strengths and opportunities. Part of my work is to figure out how they reinforce and strengthen each other. How do we take what is a really deep, rich historical model of how to educate both educators and children and make it accessible and available to a broader range of communities? If you can afford to pay $40,000 for our school or $60,000 to come to our graduate school, you're going to get a great education, the gold standard. But most people can't afford that. So how do we translate this model to something that is accessible and usable in the average school here in the city and around the country?

We have done a lot of work addressing this question. For example, we've had a big project with New York City. As the Department of Education has expanded pre-kindergarten classes to accommodate all children in the city, we have trained and provided a professional hub for many of the teachers.

Before I came to Bank Street, I had spent a lot of time trying to figure out how to change outcomes for kids in the K-12 system, but I hadn't really understood the power of early childhood. I left my job as senior deputy chancellor at the New York City Department of Education really worried about the fact that even though we saw big gains in graduation rates and fewer dropouts, the achievement gap between rich and poor kids, and between black and white kids, had stayed almost exactly where it had been when we started.

Recent breakthroughs in neuroscience suggest that a lot of the achievement gap the public schools and K-12 education system are struggling to address is rooted in what happens in the first three years of life. Those are the years when your brain is developing most rapidly. If you have the opportunity to be in an environment where you're loved and cared for—with responsive adults who talk to you and are trying to understand what's happening with you and encourage you to explore—your brain is going to develop and flourish. You will be positioned well when you start school to engage in all kinds of more sophisticated work. If you're not, if no one's talking to you, no one's telling you stories, no one's stimulating your capacities—if you're ignored, if you're abused, if you're neglected—you're much more likely to enter school with your brain already wired in ways that make it much harder to succeed.

That damage can be reversed in good schools, but it's much harder at that point than it is in the first three years. New York City has $25 billion invested each year in the K-12 system, and spends well below one-tenth of that on children before they enter school. This indicates a profound misunderstanding of the developmental needs of human beings.

There are historical reasons why it has evolved that way. But if you were to start over and think about where you would want to put your money, it's much, much better spent in the first three years than at any other point. However, today, in 2017, we have minimal infrastructure and systems to support families and young children. If you're born poor, you are likely to be cared for in an informal care setting that's very lightly regulated. Educators working in those settings typically have no instructional training or support around what kids need to develop their brains, to develop their capacity to self-regulate, to learn language, and so on.

So that's a gap. There is as yet no intentional set of public policies to address that gap, but it's starting to become a priority. The pre-kindergarten work in New York City is an example of the priorities starting to shift, but what we're doing here in the United States is 20 to 30 years behind what most other developed countries are doing. That keeps me up at night. If you look at Europe, Australia, even Canada, the investments that are made routinely in both parents and children in those first three years, they are totally different.

There are lots of small examples here, nonprofits or hospitals or other kinds of organizations that are doing good work. It means taking care of mothers as they're going through the prenatal phase, so they understand what's coming and what supports they're going to need. It means having systems in place as parents are going through that first phase after birth, to help give them advice and support. It means real public funding for child care, at a level that attracts talented people and keeps and trains them to do that work.

You get paid more as a dog walker here in New York City than as someone who works with infants in child care. That is partially because child care has been defined for so long as not being real work, and there have been strong conservative interests who didn't want public investment because they worried it would erode the family's role. But the truth is most parents are working. Where are the babies? Look for them. Are they being well taken care of? If they're poor, in most cases, the answer is no.

What is your definition of happiness, or, what is your philosophy of life?

I like the essay by Albert Camus, "The Myth of Sisyphus," which is a retelling of the myth of the guy who is condemned to continually roll the boulder up the hill. Once he gets to the top, it rolls all the way back down and he has to start over. Camus' telling of it involves reflection. What is happening to him when he's walking down the mountain? At that moment, he is not rolling the boulder and has time to think and reflect on what is happening in his life, on what it means. In what seems to be a case of someone imprisoned in a cycle that doesn't have an end, he finds hope. He has the capacity of a human being to imagine something different and to make sense of the world around him.

I think that's a really powerful lesson, because there is a lot of despair out in the world. It can feel at times that despite great efforts, there isn't much progress. Ultimately, we are free to imagine something different and, in doing so, give meaning to what we're doing. That's what matters, that action of giving meaning to the world around us.

What is the greatest misconception about you?

One of my roles when I was at the Department of Education was running the accountability system for the schools, which was based on Mayor Bloomberg's idea that you could measure success in education and in so doing improve the quality. The system generated a lot of resistance from teachers and others in the system. It was focused on a very narrow set of indicators like test scores. The tests are not that good, so they don't fully measure what kids are learning. The tests also put a lot of pressure on the folks in schools to try to get better at helping kids pass the tests, instead of focusing on educating them well.

As someone who comes out of a progressive tradition that doesn't see standardized testing as a core way to drive learning, running that accountability system was an odd position to be in. I took the job because I believed that to have an impact at a large scale, you needed to be willing to understand the details of how systems work. You need to understand how they play out from an idea at the leadership level to the experience of someone in a school, in a classroom. In the choices you make as you take an idea through those different steps, there's lots of space to innovate and create room for educators to do creative, thoughtful work. So I saw my job at that time as trying to build a really good version of that system, even though I had real questions about some of the consequences of our work.

In the political fights that occurred between the Bloomberg administration and the union and other activists in the education space, there was often a binary discourse that developed around both sides, one side demonizing the other unfairly and polarizing the discourse to organize people around one perspective or the other. Being in the middle of that political fight meant that I was perceived to be on one side of the equation, even though there were times when I didn't agree with the policies that I was charged with upholding and times when the policies themselves were misunderstood just because of where they originated.

What is the most important thing you tell young people who are thinking about making careers in the nonprofit sector?

I've been thinking a lot about why fewer people are going into teaching. Graduate schools around the country have seen a 40 percent decline in the last seven or eight years of folks going into teaching. I think part of the reason is there are other interesting jobs, for example, in the tech sector. I just had a meeting the other day at Google. Google is filled with 20-somethings who are smart and interested in changing the world and making a lot more money than they could make as teachers and in much less stressful conditions.

There is a more diverse range of opportunities available to folks at this moment than there were 10 or 20 years ago. But there are also a lot of for-profit businesses that have taken on the mantle of social impact as a way to attract talent. Sometimes those businesses do actually try to have an impact. It's not always disingenuous. But having a real impact, like doing social change that leads to real change, is usually not as easy as we'd like it to be.

So you have to make choices in your life about where you want to put your talent and your energy. It's important to be honest about those choices. I have no problem with someone who wants to make money or do something that is rooted in skills that will take them far away from working with people. But I think there's also something really powerful in working with people and figuring out how to do that well. That's part of what a career in education is focused on. It can connect to some of our aspirations. A lot of people today do have real aspirations to change the world. So work like teaching, which is really challenging and really difficult to do well, is an important thing to do.

A 2016 U.S. Trust study shows that high net worth Americans have greater confidence in individuals and nonprofits than in the executive branch or Congress. With the current administration and Congress, what role should the nonprofit sector and organizations like yours play over the next several years?

I think the reason for that lack of confidence is that the work of reforming public bureaucracies into high functioning organizations is slow and doesn't happen within the regular election cycle. Given the election cycle, most public bureaucracies never change.

Take school systems as an example. The average super-intendent lasts just under three years. That's not enough time to actually do anything. People end up leaving those jobs, because the minute you try to engage in meaningful reform, you inevitably upset someone. In a governance structure where the local school board is turning over every two to four years, it's easy to organize and get seats on that board if your constituency is not happy with the superintendent.

So you have this revolving door that means that there's very little change. If you want to stay longer, it's only safe to make very small adjustments. There are rare cases—and New York City was one of them—where there is less vulner-ability to the governance structure. When Bloomberg came into office, he got mayoral control of the schools. He didn't have any allegiances to the political machine in the city. So he was able to give his chancellor freedom to restructure the organization and make a lot of changes.

Interestingly though, many of those changes were reversed after he left office. Not all of them, but a lot of those changes were changed back. There's a lot of built in stasis that makes it really difficult to sustain high-quality work inside a bureaucracy.

I think it's possible, just very complicated. I'm inter-ested in trying to figure out how to do more of that kind of work, because I saw the kinds of progress we started to make in New York City. So it's definitely doable, but how you structure the transitions between different administrations and how you protect strong leaders so change can actually happen is a challenge.

If there is one thing you could say to your colleagues who are leading grant-making foundations, what would that be?

I think there's a similar risk in the cycle that nonprofits have with foundations. Typically, the timelines for success are pegged to the life of the grant, and that's usually not enough time to actually do the work and sustain it so that it is successful. It is important to think about ways to stretch that out. It is also important to think about ways to measure success differently.

That's partially driven by folks at the federal level. There has been this fascination with randomized control trials and other kinds of hard quantitative evidence of work in the nonprofit sector, to prove something is worth investing in. The truth is that that type of research, which was designed primarily for medical purposes, isn't so useful in work with organizations and people, because it requires you to fix a set of conditions in place—even as you realize as you're working on a project that you've made a mistake and need to change things. It is hard to get a statistically significant impact, and even those impacts actually are relatively tiny. Those impacts are not enough to really move the needle in the way that we would need to move it to get the kind of deep change that's required. The more iterative approach to measuring effectiveness, similar to what you see in the tech world—where there are lots of opportunities to fail and find the wrong path and also opportunities to find the right path—is much more likely to succeed. At this point, that's not how the majority of funders think about the work.

CHAPTER 3

Nonet Sykes

Director of Racial and Ethnic Equity and Inclusion, The Annie E. Casey Foundation

As director of racial and ethnic equity and inclusion at the Annie E. Casey Foundation, Nonet Sykes identifies, implements and promotes the most effective strategies to increase equitable opportunities and outcomes for children, families and communities of color. She serves as a member of the racial equity and leadership advisory board of the National League of Cities, as a member of the equity advisory committee of the Opportunity Finance Network, as a board member of the National Recreation and Parks Association, and as a board member of the Association of Baltimore Area Grantmakers (ABAG). She also serves as co-chair of ABAG's Equity, Diversity and Inclusion Committee. Sykes holds a B.S. from the University of Maryland Eastern Shore, a master of public administration from the University of Baltimore, and a Certificate in Organizational Consulting and Change Leadership from Georgetown University.

The Annie E. Casey Foundation

The Annie E. Casey Foundation is devoted to developing a brighter future for millions of children at risk of poor educational, economic, social and health outcomes in the United States. Its work focuses on strengthening families, building stronger communities and ensuring access to opportunity, because children need all three to succeed. It advances research and solutions to overcome the barriers to success, help communities demonstrate what works and influence decision makers to invest in strategies based on solid evidence.

As a private philanthropy based in Baltimore that works nationwide, it awards grants to help federal agencies, states, counties, cities and neighborhoods create more innovative, cost-effective responses to issues negatively affecting children: poverty, unnecessary disconnection from family, and communities with limited access to opportunity. Since 1948, these efforts have translated into more informed policies and practices and yielded positive results for larger numbers of kids and families.

Nonet Sykes

At what point in your life did you realize that you wanted to build your career in the nonprofit sector? Why did you make this commitment?

I think I always wanted to be in a helping profession. I received my undergraduate degree in rehabilitation services, with the hope that I was going to be doing some sort of rehab or occupational therapy. As an undergrad, I did an internship with a community medical rehabilitation center, and I fell in love with the fact that I was providing firsthand support to community members who didn't have access to other kinds of health care services.

I then went to graduate school with the intention of getting a master's in public administration in health care administration. I was offered a Housing and Urban Development fellowship that would pay for my graduate school expenses, but required me to concentrate on community and economic development rather than health care administration. I immediately went to work for a community development financial institution that focused on providing loans and credit access to small minority businesses in Baltimore City.

After about seven years doing community development, I joined the Casey Foundation in 2001 as a program associate, supporting the foundation's most significant multi-site community-change initiative, focused on improving outcomes for kids and families living in tough neighborhoods. I've stayed in the nonprofit sector space for my entire career. I really didn't think about it. It felt quite natural to me from the very beginning.

What was your proudest moment in the sector?

It was when the president of our foundation decided to make racial and ethnic equity and inclusion a foundation priority. We've always had staff members who were championing equity, diversity and inclusion, but in 2014, we wrote and launched the *Race for Results* report, which had such a great reaction in the field. The positive response from the field about that report, along with all the internal conversations we had leading up to that, led our foundation president to state strongly that we would never be able to achieve our foundation's mission if we didn't pay close attention to racial equity.

I was very proud that the foundation leadership wanted to create this report that explicitly named race as the leading barrier to successful outcomes. I was even more proud when our foundation president said it would be a priority for us, because this work is so critical and essential for us to achieve our mission.

Thus far, what have been the worst and best events in your life, and what did those experiences teach you?

The worst thing that happened to me was experiencing some very serious medical issues. I had a period of about three years where I was having unexplained seizures. It was a very scary and tough time. I went through years of testing, including sleep studies, brain monitoring, CAT scans and EEGs, to figure out what was going on, but nobody could tell me what it was. All the reports were normal, which was even more frightening. I was at Johns Hopkins Hospital for an entire week, undergoing brain monitoring. They found no abnormal brain waves. My seizures only occurred at night, while sleeping, so I stayed overnight several times, but never had one seizure. None of these top neurologists could tell me anything. Finally, my primary care physician suggested I see a doctor who practiced alternative medicine. It was there that she started asking me questions about what was going on right up until I started having the seizures. She quickly figured out that they were all stress-related.

Before the first seizure, I was planning a wedding, building a house, selling a house, and renovating one to get tenants to live in it. There was a lot going on, and I had a pretty demanding job. My brain was constantly processing at night when I was ready to lie down. I was going through the mental checklist of all the things I needed to do, and my brain couldn't handle it anymore. I lost my driving privileges and was totally dependent on my family to get me everywhere. I was miserable, because I was always in control, independent, and never dependent on anybody for anything.

I married my husband in December, and my seizures started in February. It was a lot to be newlyweds in a new home, experiencing this health crisis. It was a moment for me of having deep faith that God would pull me through, and learning to let go of things I couldn't control. I had to become OK with having to rely on other people. I had the last seizure in January of 2007, and have been seizure-free for more than a decade.

The best thing that happened to me is my family. I have an incredible family. They are awesome, including everyone from my grandmother to my parents, my siblings, my children and my husband, who never once wavered in his commitment to our marriage and our vows, through sickness and health. I got pregnant with my first child in the midst of all the seizures. I was taking all kinds of different medications and wasn't sure if or how it would affect the baby. I was constantly praying that we would both be fine. It was awesome to know I could rely on my family to be there no matter what.

If tragedy struck and you couldn't do this kind of work as of tomorrow, what's the single most important piece of advice you would have for the next person to step into your shoes?

Lean into the role and use it to your fullest. Don't shy away from the commitment to take on racial and ethnic equity and inclusion work. That's the single most important issue of our time. Given the recent election results, I think some people are worried that we just regressed 50 years. Step into this space and embrace it with open arms. Don't be confined by the title or the role. Lean in with the audacity of ambition, and use all of your power and your role to your fullest potential and capacity.

What is your definition of happiness?

Happiness is being at peace. So much of my day is spent juggling internal and external efforts, thinking strategically, and trying to balance work and home. My kids always ask me what I want for my birthday or Christmas. I say, "I just want peace." It's about peace within and peace around me. That's what brings me happiness.

What's the most important thing you tell young people who are thinking about making careers in the nonprofit sector?

I tell them that this is their moment, and that they need to think big and bold, and not second-guess themselves. Because I was young when I entered this field, many people assumed I didn't have knowledge or expertise. They almost made me feel like I didn't belong here, but I knew I had similar or greater credentials than many of the people I was working with.

Young people should remember that they were hired for a reason, based on skills and experience. Don't second-guess why you're there. Be fully present and lean into that. When you come with your ambition, make sure you have done your research and you have data. So much of what we do in philanthropy is based on data. You must have data to support your ideas and strategies. Also, find other allies in this space, and do some bridge-building to bring everyone together, rather than creating more division between racial and ethnic groups.

What new opportunities do you see for Annie E. Casey in the next five years?

I see us applying our racial and ethnic equity and inclusion knowledge, tools and strategies more precisely to our work over the next few years, with much better understanding and articulation of root causes.

We'll also be testing out our messaging strategies, like how to articulate our commitments around racial and ethnic equity. Finally, we will also be implementing an equity score-card. That will allow us to track and measure our progress towards operationalizing the foundation's commitment to equity and inclusion across five core areas—programmatic strategy, governance, operations, human resources, and investments. We plan to collect data annually and provide a written report every two years that will be shared with our board of trustees, senior leadership and staff and posted on our website. The findings will be reviewed by our board and senior leaders, who will implement plans to address any shortcomings that will be identified by the scorecard.

Moving our work forward in this way will allow the Annie E. Casey Foundation to have a culture that normalizes con-versations about racial equity and organizes the institution to achieve racial and ethnic equity and inclusion internally and throughout our programmatic and grant-making strategies.

If you could invite five living people to a meeting to have a discussion that would change how the nonprofit sector evolves over the next five years, whom would you invite to that conversation, and what would you talk about?

The person at the top of my list would be Angela Glover Blackwell. She's the CEO at PolicyLink. I find her to be incred-ibly thoughtful and inspiring. She's been doing this work for 35 years and has seen a lot. She knows the importance of pol-icy as a leader for systems change and instructional change. She understands the importance of racial equity. She's very forward-thinking. Angela was talking about equity being a superior growth model for our nation's economy more than five years ago.

john powell [*Editor's note: john prefers to use lowercase in his name*] is the second person. He's the director of the Haas Institute for a Fair and Inclusive Society at the University of California at Berkeley. john's a racial equity scholar who has also been around for a long time, advancing racial equity and researching structural racism and implicit bias. He's brilliant in this space. He's focused on building more bridges as a nation and inviting everybody into what he calls "the circle of human concern." The 2016 election elevated the divisiveness and the view of people of color, LGBTQ people and immigrants as the "other." john has been strategizing how to encourage empathy, stop seeing marginalized groups as "the other," and help everybody see us all as belonging in this space together.

Another person is Glenn Harris. He's the CEO of Race Forward, based in New York. Glenn just managed a merger of two of the country's leading racial justice organizations to advance systemic racial equity in organizing, journalism, government, philanthropy and other fields.

How are the choices of the wealthy private philanthropists influencing traditional foundation giving?

Philanthropy is a field where we can be bold and take risks. Philanthropists should understand that equity is needed, especially within the education system. I think there is a real opportunity for more strategy and intentionality when it comes to focusing on equity in education. Unfortunately, the current education system doesn't work for the majority of the kids, especially kids of color. Casey is not an education funder, but ensuring that all children can attend a high-quality, inclusive school where they can learn and thrive is important. Everyone is touched by the education system, and education is hugely important in putting everyone on a path to success.

What is the one thing you would say to your colleagues who are leading nonprofits seeking foundation funding?

I'd say to be thoughtful and clear about the outcomes you seek and the impact you want to achieve through your organization. Be prepared to provide data that shows you are achieving those outcomes. Nonprofits must be comfortable with data. Both quantitative and qualitative data are extremely helpful, to know whether your strategies are making a difference. Data also helps you to get to the right strategies faster. Also, I think a lot of nonprofits spend so much time chasing money that they don't have time to actually do the good work they've received money for. When all you do is run around asking for more money, but you don't deliver by the time your grant is up, you're not likely to get funded again. Be thoughtful about how you use your time, and make sure you do what you said you were going to do with the money you were given.

What was the biggest lesson you ever learned in hiring or letting people go?

I would say the biggest lesson is to trust your gut and keep the lines of communication open. When you're managing people, you have to be able to provide authentic feedback along the way, so that the staff you are managing know where they stand and how they are doing. Don't wait for an annual performance review. Check in with staff regularly to help them understand where they are doing well and where they can grow.

CHAPTER 4

Bill Ulfelder

*New York Executive Director,
The Nature Conservancy*

Bill Ulfelder leads the Nature Conservancy's New York program, with a staff of 140 people and more than 70,000 members, including 100 trustees across the state. In 2012, he helped launch the Conservancy's first urban conservation program in New York City. Today, the New York City program is focused on coastal resilience work to protect the communities around New York City from the threats of sea-level rise and significant weather events. With more than half of the world's population living in cities, protecting cities is essential. The Nature Conservancy is addressing climate change in cities and furthering urban conservation through natural infrastructure, science-based strategies and smart policy.

Ulfelder's education background includes a prestigious Morehead-Cain Scholarship at the University of North Carolina at Chapel Hill, during which he spent time studying conservation in the Peruvian Amazon. Upon graduation, he was awarded a Fulbright Scholarship to undertake a work-study program with the Panamanian Park Service, before earning dual master's degrees from Duke University Nicholas School of the Environment in resource economics and policy, as well as forest management.

He joined the Conservancy in 1995, when he was awarded a Population and Environment Fellowship with the University of Michigan, which provided him with the opportunity to work with the Conservancy in Peru and Ecuador.

In 1997, Ulfelder was appointed Peru program director, where he helped negotiate a $10.5 million debt-for-nature swap that provides income for Peruvian protected areas. In 2003, he moved to Flagstaff, Arizona, where he served as the Conservancy's Northern Arizona director, overseeing forest conservation efforts with the U.S. Forest Service and conservation and community interests. As the Conservancy's Eastern Colorado director, he oversaw grasslands conservation of the Western High Plains and led numerous partnership efforts within both the private and public sectors. Additionally, he served as the Conservancy's Central Caribbean director, leading conservation efforts in the Dominican Republic, Haiti, Cuba and Puerto Rico for much of 2008.

The Nature Conservancy

The Nature Conservancy is a global conservation organization dedicated to conserving the lands and waters on which all life depends. Guided by science, it creates innovative, on-the-ground solutions to the world's toughest challenges, so that nature and people can thrive together. It tackles climate change, conserving lands, waters and oceans at an unprecedented scale, and helping make cities more sustainable. Working in more than 65 countries, it uses a collaborative approach that engages local communities, governments, the private sector and other partners.

Bill Ulfelder

Who has had the greatest influence on you as a professional?

I've been incredibly blessed, and an important element of my success is that I've had different mentors at different times throughout my career, from when I was a brand-new employee, just out of graduate school, through today. They've all been so important to me in different ways and so selfless in their support. The person that jumps to mind is Roger Milliken Jr., who was for many years the global chair of the Nature Conservancy. I had the opportunity to connect with him, and we got to know each other quite well. I really appreciated the time I spent learning from him as a human being, a conservationist and a business leader.

I would also say, unabashedly, my wife, who I met at the Nature Conservancy 20 years ago when she worked there. She understands that culture: the people and the leaders who are still around. Modesty aside, I think of those great presidential biographies that talk about the roles their spouses played in their lives. I would say I've known my wife nearly as long as I've worked with the Nature Conservancy, and that has been an incredibly important relationship and influence throughout my career.

Thus far, what have been the worst and best events in your life, and what did those experiences teach you?

When I was hired for the New York executive director job in 2008, I was not fully qualified for the magnitude of it. I was incredibly naive, and I took the job from Colorado, in the midst of the global economic meltdown. I had no idea what was coming. For the first couple of years, I thought things were going well. There was a moment where I sought to consolidate units within the Nature Conservancy, including their voluntary leader boards, do away with some senior leader staff and turn over leadership. To this day, I think the principle of what I was doing, in a pure sense, was right. I thought that through charm, and talking to folks, I'd win them over and ultimately get what I wanted. It resulted in a nuclear catastrophe. People were really upset, and that reached the global CEO of the Nature Conservancy. It was a humiliating management and strategic disaster that was a result of my having been raised with a different leadership model. I call it the hero model, which is to be the smartest person in the room, have all the right answers, and see everyone through it.

It sent me down a hole over a series of years, and as a result I had to reconsider my management approach. I started with the more traditional leadership training facilities, like the Center for Creative Leadership in Colorado Springs, which I think is one of the best in the country. It was still too close, in certain ways, to the old way of doing business. We've come to use an organization which is working at the highest levels of the Nature Conservancy now, called Conversant. They have a different leadership model, which is about contributive design making. It's not democracy or consensus. In a sense, it's benevolent dictatorship, in that you give the right people the opportunity to provide input and guidance. Even if you don't do what they're suggesting, they know they've had an audience and that you paid close attention to what they said, and that the ultimate decision, as a result of that process, is better informed. It's been a big switch. It was an embarrassing professional experience, but out of it came a whole other journey. New York is now a successful unit within the Nature Conservancy, and I attribute it to that disaster.

Another experience was when I first started out in the organization. I had a two-year fellowship in Ecuador, and during that time, two of my first three mentors were diagnosed with cancer. They both subsequently died, and that was really hard for me, because they meant so much to me as colleagues and friends, and I had to grow as a leader really fast.

What, if anything, keeps you up at night?

There are two things I think about a lot these days. One is: How does the Nature Conservancy, a nonpartisan, nonconfrontational, big-tent organization, succeed with its conservation agenda in these challenging times? The vast majority of environmental organizations have chosen sides. They criticize the administration, and these are great organizations, with many of my own friends and colleagues, whom I support. The Nature Conservancy is proudly nonpartisan, so our challenge is effectively engaging where there are opportunities, and protecting the safeguards that are so important to the economy, well-being, health and prosperity of the United States. We're thinking about how many resources we should dedicate at the federal level, which is getting all the news and attention. We're also thinking about how much we should dedicate at the state level, which is where the real action is.

The Nature Conservancy is continually changing. We launched a successful campaign almost two years ago, but our vision for the future, which was the foundation for the campaign, has evolved since then. So how do we make this successful evolution from the old to the new? How do we keep donors, trustees and supporters feeling excited about where we're going? We're appropriately taking on new challenges and thinking about new ways to do business. How do we manage that strategic shift and make sure we're being financially responsible and sustainable? Those are the biggest things I'm thinking of these days.

What is your definition of happiness, or, what is your philosophy of life?

I ask myself if I'm making a difference. It feels really good to make a difference and work in a sector that I know not only has the intention of making a difference, but where I actually see the differences we're making. My connection to my family and open communication with them is also important. If you wait to build your family time during spring breaks or sabbaticals, you've lost the opportunity to be deeply connected to your family. A lot of my dealings with Roger Milliken have been about how I want to show up as a husband to my wife and a father to my daughter. I realized that I need to prioritize work less and focus on my family, because that would ultimately allow me to be a better leader and more successful at work.

What is the greatest misconception about you?

I think people believe that I come from a background of incredible privilege. There are certain things in my life that suggest that. I went to prep school in New England. I attended the University of North Carolina, Chapel Hill, where I played lacrosse. I went to Duke. My father is a trustee of the Nature Conservancy. But it's actually more complicated than that. My parents divorced when I was 3 years old, so while my father's family came from considerable means, my brother and I grew up as kids of a young, working, divorced mom. It was tough, and we had a lot of lean years. I would spend August at my father's grandparents' place, overlooking the bay of the South Shore in Massachusetts. But in New York, our means were nowhere near what folks imagine. So I think I surprised people with my appreciation and understanding of what it means to be from different classes, because they had no idea that I had a dual experience growing up.

I think it makes me a much more effective fund-raiser, because I'm neither one nor the other. Growing up in two worlds broadened my mind, and it made me appreciate different ways of thinking about money and resources, and charity. You're a more effective leader when you've been challenged to think differently at different times, and have different perspectives. Exposure to different cultures and classes gives you more appreciation for just how different they are, and you become more effective at solving things on their own terms.

What is the most important thing you tell young people who are thinking about making careers in the nonprofit sector?

Multilingualism, multilingualism, multilingualism. Go see other cultures, travel the country, leave the country, have those experiences. The other thing that I coach them on is to make themselves known. People are more likely to hire somebody they've actually met and are impressed by, so find a way to make yourself known. Volunteer, show up and know that it's a bit of a long game.

I've come to emphasize the nonlinear nature of careers. People often ask how I got to where I am. It was a circuitous journey. Someone once introduced me saying I was going to talk about my career and my upward and lateral moves. I added that I'd also talk about my backward moves, because there was a moment where I was in a senior leadership position at the Nature Conservancy, and my wife and I decided we wanted to move west. I took a job in Flagstaff, Arizona. I took a huge pay cut, and I was reporting to somebody who reported to a senior leader in the organization. People might have seen that as moving two steps down rather than up, but it felt right at the time, and as a result, I got to know a person who then hired me into the Colorado chapter and has played a big role in my learning and ascension in the organization. It was a great decision. My deputy at the time called it a strategic retreat, and I think people need to be aware that these "retreats" are nonlinear, but can be immensely educational and informative in the long run. I look back at some of my experiences and internships that I thought were disastrous at the time, and I realize I needed to have those experiences to gain clarification and go in a different direction. So, embrace the experiences as they emerge, and the lessons will emerge from those moments and long afterward.

How important is it to find the right people for your board? What qualities do you seek, and how successful have you been at matching those qualities?

The board is fundamental. My proudest accomplishment as the New York executive director was taking a board that was punching below its weight class and turning it into one that is far more dynamic, engaged, diverse and philanthropic than anyone could have imagined it would be eight years ago. Strategic direction, surrounding myself with an incredibly capable, diverse executive team, and a strong board are the highest priorities for me. I think about it every day.

We have a young, energetic, dynamic board that really represents where the Nature Conservancy is going in terms of people and nature. They see the well-being of humanity as a fundamental element of what the Nature Conservancy does. Now we're talking about adding to the board. The Nature Conservancy has a program called Leaders for Environmental Action for the Future (LEAF), where we take city youth at environmentally themed high schools and give them paid summer internships. That serves as the door opener to their getting college scholarships, and maybe even graduate school scholarships and then a career. It may not be a career in conservation, but the idea is for them to bring this ethic with them. We're getting ready to create a position on our board for a LEAF alum, so somebody who's just finished school and doesn't yet have philanthropic capacity can have the opportunity to learn about charities, nonprofit management and serving on a board. It's also an opportunity for trustees to learn from them.

I feel really good about where we are, but I'm never complacent. The job is never done, and I'm always thinking about succession and what the board might be missing. I need to have a great working relationship with the individual trustees, and it's important that the group has a good dynamic. I've started to hear about our trustees getting together outside of board meetings. They've gone on bike rides in Boca on spring break, or they've run into each other in Aspen, and they go skiing together. Those instances tell me that this is working. We're building the kind of community that we wanted to create, and they're seizing upon it. It's really rewarding to me.

What new opportunities do you see for your organization in the next five years?

No. 1 is changing the Nature Conservancy's mission from being strictly nature or biodiversity-focused to conserving the lands and waters on which all life depends. It's more of a statement about the well-being of humanity, and we've opened ourselves to that as we're thinking about connections to public health and economic well-being, whether it's in New York City or rural communities. Because we can't be masters of everything, we have to seek the most effective partnerships. We just created one with Pathfinder International in East Africa. They're a great family-planning and maternal and child health organization. We're not experts in that area, so we're just now beginning to wrap our heads around all of these opportunities, and I have no doubt that it's going to lead to big, significant things.

Another opportunity is in cities. New York City was the first to create a comprehensive urban conservation program. We started working on it before Hurricane Sandy, and then when that hit, the board rallied around the program. Today it's not a huge team, but it's grown significantly in the last few years. I think it's a good opportunity to be in cities, engaging with large audiences and educating them about the Nature Conservancy close to where they live. We were quietly conserving nature for too long, and we missed a lot of opportunities. Now we're building awareness about who we are, and we're starting to do that in New York City. We're seeing big changes in recognition and traffic to our website, and even some increases in donations.

After the 2016 election, *The New York Times* reported, "the widening political divergence between cities and small-town America also reflects a growing alienation between the two groups, and a sense—perhaps accurate—that their fates are not connected." What role should the nonprofit sector play in helping the two groups find common ground?

We are a global organization, working in 69 different countries around the world. We have staff and volunteer leaders in every state, so it's a pretty broad spectrum. Our Mississippi board leans to the right, and our New York board leans to the left, yet they're both part of the Nature Conservancy. More people are moving out of rural areas and into big cities, so they're getting exposed to diversity, and their tolerance grows, but it's important to never underestimate what a small group of politically motivated people can do. I think there's work to be done, and the nonprofit sectors, specifically the Nature Conservancy, are well poised, because we are talking and listening to both sides, and trying to find the place where we can work together.

About a year ago, I was sitting at a table with trustees from left-leaning states like New York and Washington, as well as right-leaning states like Nebraska and Alaska. Within the first 20 minutes of the conversation, people were arguing about climate change. People from New York and Washington were pushing science and data, but people from Kansas and Alaska don't even use the term "climate change." So we had to find where the mutual interests were. For Kansas, that meant talking about supporting an agrarian way of life. Families have been leaving their farms and ranches, but renewable energy and wind turbines can put money in the pockets of farmers and ranchers, which would allow them to stay on these farms. Once we sold renewable energy as something advantageous, in ways other than reducing fossil-fuel emissions, we got them interested. Meanwhile, back in New York, we can keep talking about climate change. It goes back to effective leadership. Bringing a diverse group together means making everyone feel included and that they have a voice, so everyone can work together. It's about using the right language and finding a respectful, thoughtful way to have the conversation.

We're in the midst of a national conversation about race and racial equity. What is your organization doing both internally and externally to address racial inequity?

I would say the work is more internal right now. The Nature Conservancy is a disproportionately white organization, and there is a growing awareness about the value of being more diverse in terms of ethnicity, socioeconomics and gender. We're on a learning road, and we have a long way to go. I think it has a lot to do with leadership at the top setting an example and listening to the younger, shorter-tenured trustees who bring a whole different mindset, and challenge the old-guard leadership. It hasn't translated well into our external partnerships, so in New York, we're going to spend a couple of years working with staff internally, and then move on to the board. We've opened our first diversity discussion with a panel of trustees, talking to them about their experiences as female scientists, female political organizers, women in the financial sector and women of color. Once we've made real progress with the board, then we'll move on to external partnerships. It'll take time and will require a different skill set, so that's what we need to focus on.

My advice to anyone trying to create a more diverse staff would be to hire a consultant who knows more than you do. That's what we did. We hired a consultant who runs a company called SoulFire Consulting, and she's been working with us for about three years. It was a slow start, but we've seen an increase in awareness.

With this new administration and Congress, what role should the nonprofit sector and organizations like the Nature Conservancy play in the next two to four years?

Given the total polarization of the United States, it's easy to just stay in your tribe, listen to feedback in whatever your bubble is, whether that's the New York City progressive bubble or the right-leaning bubble. We need to find ways to connect, open dialogues and work through the biases, whether they're unconscious or conscious, for real substance and outcomes that are going to serve the country in the long term. I think that's the power of our current political situation, that we have the opportunity to do that.

What is one thing you would tell your colleagues who are leading grant-making foundations?

I love the debate and pushback people are giving around the overhead question and the administrative costs. There are some real nonprofit leaders out there making clear that what you really need to look at are organizational impacts rather than getting hung up on figures. Focus on impact. Investing in your staff training and modernization are so fundamental to remaining innovative and creative. Don't take your eye off the right ball, which is really about the impact.

I love the idea of unconventional partnerships with other organizations, and working together to do more. I think there are a lot of opportunities to do more and make a bigger impact if we work with unusual partners like, say, Planned Parenthood. It'll take a long time to get it right, but it doesn't mean there can't be impact indicators along the way. I think the impact indicators are more important than the process indicators, and just slowing down to understand that is key.

CHAPTER 5

Ensure Your Own House Is in Order

Now you have sharpened your leadership skills and are ready to set up your own organization for success. According to many of our interviewees, this is a prerequisite to effecting positive social change.

Many books have been written on organizational culture and change management. This is not one of them. However, from our interviews, we identified five practices that distinguish many of the organizations our interviewees lead.

A. Recruit Talented, Passionate Employees, Preferably Ones Who Are Smarter Than You

Our interviewees agree that finding talented employees is one of the most important and difficult tasks for their organizations.

Michael Capasso, general director of New York City Opera, says, "I want to be surrounded by smart board members and staff. Everybody on my staff is smarter than I am, and I'm not ashamed of it. People in leadership roles have to be able to surround themselves with a cabinet of people to whom they will listen."

At least one-third of our leaders work in the nonprofit sector because they benefited when they were growing up from services that nonprofits provide. Brian Gallagher's family used food stamps and went to social workers. Tara Perry, CEO of the National CASA (Court Appointed Special Advocates for Children) was herself a foster child.

In other cases, the parents of our leaders worked in the sector or volunteered actively. Kathy Calvin, CEO of the United Nations Foundation, recalls, "My mother was in the nonprofit sector, but as a volunteer. I look back now and think, 'Well, she was onto something,' and she probably instilled something in me that made me think there's a value to finding purpose and service in whatever one does."

Fred Blackwell, CEO of the San Francisco Foundation, remembers: "On my mother's side, I come from a family of people who are nonprofit professionals and community organizers. From a very early age, I was exposed to this part of the world of work. I was exposed to concepts of social justice and economic justice. I went to the school founded by the Black Panther Party in Oakland, California."

From a management perspective, this merits some consideration. In corporations, applicants for employment are usually drawn from a pool of the technically skilled and professionally qualified. Rarely these days are they following a career path modeled by a family member or someone with whom they have personal ties.

Recruitment in the nonprofit world is difficult partially because it doesn't match the "Post and fill" approach to a job search that corporate and government recruitment survive on. Yet this is the way workers are matched with the roles nonprofits need to fill.

Finding skilled, talented and experienced talent for nonprofits has often been done the wrong way, adopting the "warm body for the moment" approach typical of modern business and government. Instead, new tools and approaches of reaching potential nonprofit sector workers best suited to work in nonprofit organizations need to be the focus of recruiting, starting in high school. The sector could benefit from long-term talent development and recruitment strategies. We need to think of the nonprofit sector as a career choice, not just as a transition between jobs.

Tara Perry is concerned about staff turnover, which is as challenging in the nonprofit sector as it is in the private sector. She is determined to keep her employees motivated and engaged so that she doesn't lose the best talent. She believes it is best to be up front with people who are considering work in nonprofit organizations. You have to tell them, she says, that the work is hard, and that they won't get rich.

Perry's technique is to use multiple interviews. She has found that candidates who are willing to show up for a series of meetings are more likely to be ready when the time comes to commit to a job in the nonprofit sector, not just to accept a job because they need employment.

Perry's techniques are worth noting. As we observed earlier, attracting talent to the sector is another challenge nonprofits must overcome to get and keep the people they need. Someone may express interest in a job in your organization without really understanding what it means to work in a nonprofit.

Since the work requires persistence and patience, it makes sense that the job interview process also requires persistence and patience. If candidates show up to several interviews, even without a clear understanding of why they are being asked back so many times, the organization can get a sense of the dedication they are likely to display toward their work if they are hired.

Responding to the high turnover among the younger generation in the job market, our interviewees have some advice about the value of staying power. Kevin Washington, CEO of the YMCA of the USA, suggests, "Too often, young people are looking at the next job. I tell them to focus on the current job. People are always watching you. Focus on the job at hand, and you will get noticed."

Stacy Palmer, editor of *The Chronicle of Philanthropy*, says that she has found that some millennials will tell her, "I had six or seven bosses in the last year, or in the last two years." She asks, "How are they ever going to learn? Especially in the fund-raising field, where there's so much turnover. We must recognize what cost that is to the younger people in the profession."

Palmer points to a major concern we have. When we recruit talent for our clients, we always test their commitment to the proposed role before they get too far into the process. Sometimes, when we ask the question, "Where do you want to be in five years?" we get an honest answer, because they are taken by surprise that we are asking such an outmoded question.

B. Give Your Employees Autonomy In Decision-Making

Giving employees autonomy can be one of the most challenging skills for a new leader to learn. Many of us who have achieved positions of leadership have done so by exercising control. Letting go of some of that control can be difficult, but it is a prerequisite for achieving the next level of leadership in a complex, interconnected world. We cannot stress enough the importance of learning this skill in attracting and retaining talented staff members, especially young staff members.

We have had much success in working with young people as independent contractors on our project teams for clients. We have found that the key to this success is to treat young hires with respect, as valued team members rather than subordinates, because they bring their own special talents and perspectives to the table. Senior team members serve more as coaches to the younger team members, rather than bosses.

Shael Polakow-Suransky, president of Bank Street College of Education, describes how, early in his career, he was assigned to do an internship with the principal of a school in Queens, Eric Nadelstern. "As a leader, Nadelstern is someone who believes deeply in autonomy as one of the most important preconditions for success. Working under him, I had a tremendous amount of flexibility and freedom to figure out how to get from point A to point B. I also had a lot of clarity around what was meant by point B."

Leon Botstein, president of Bard College, has a similar view of what it means to guide a great institution. He told us, "The trick to building an organization is people, and they must be people of ambition and quality. You have to give them authority and visibility. Do not micromanage. We've been successful in this institution by recruiting first-rate people and giving them latitude, freedom, independence, autonomy and room to maneuver."

The balance between giving people autonomy and continuing to run an institution effectively is not easy to achieve. Hiring the right people is key. When we have engaged smart, motivated employees, given them clear goals, and checked in with them on a weekly or bi-weekly basis, we have been successful. When we have made hiring mistakes, as we inevitably did, our organizations have suffered until we recognized that these were not the right employees.

C. Make Organizational Culture a Priority

Organizational health is a growing preoccupation for these leaders. Ellen LaPointe, CEO of Northern California Grantmakers, which provides services to the philanthropic community, says, "Paying attention to your internal culture and community is a prerequisite for impact."

This is not just the latest fad in management. Organizations have learned that to drive social change consistently and regularly, they must pay attention to creating a nurturing, yet challenging, environment at home.

Brian Gallagher, CEO of United Way Worldwide, has recently taken steps to improve the culture of his organization. He says, "We just hired a chief culture officer. I keep hearing culture starts at the top. I know intellectually that we should celebrate. My life experience has developed in me a very strong sense of empathy. I have an innate feeling when people are hurting. I am pretty good at knowing when other people are hurting. I am not very good at celebrating the small things."

While some for-profit and nonprofit organizations continue to create shareholder value or raise philanthropic dollars even when their employees are miserable, our leaders are saying they have learned that it is too difficult to effect real social change with an organization that is not healthy.

Of course, the smartest corporations recognize the importance of culture. They promote volunteering and other kinds of employee engagement. We recently heard a speech by Richard C. Shadyac, Jr., CEO of the American Lebanese Syrian Associated Charities (ALSAC), which raises $1 billion annually to support the St. Jude Children's Research Hospital. This makes ALSAC the sixth-largest charity in the United States.

Shadyac showed a short film about a partnership between the hospital and the travel company Expedia, in which Expedia employees travel to places the patients could never go, like Argentina, and then conduct virtual tours of these places while the hospitalized children watch in 3D on large screens. This allows children who, for example, love horses, to see the horses run free on the pampas in real time. Shadyac noted that the hospital has relationships with 60 Fortune 500 companies. What is the biggest perk these companies offer their employee volunteers? It is a trip to the hospital to spend time with the kids who have cancer.

While St. Jude Children's Research Hospital is in the enviable position of raising more money than most nonprofits will ever see, its approach is instructive. We hear all the time about the importance of giving people a direct experience of your organization's mission, and its reason for existing. St. Jude's has taken this advice and made it a centerpiece of its strategy.

Another important component of culture is transparency in decision-making about large issues that affect all or most staff. Nonprofit organizations have many more stakeholders than corporations, so decision-making can take much more time. This is a frustration and a reality of working in the sector.

Tom Dente, CEO of Humentum, which trains operations professionals in international nonprofits, says, "It's not about the answer. It's about how you get to the answer, and being inclusive all the way through that journey. Bring your team, board and communities along." We observe that nonprofit leaders need much more patience than their corporate counterparts if they want to make lasting change in a sustainable way.

D. Address Diversity and Inclusion, and Keep Addressing Them

Our leaders recognize the need to address racial inequity, and almost all are taking steps to increase the conversations about race within their organizations. The nonprofit sector can be seen as both ahead of and behind the corporate and government sectors in this area. Many nonprofits have missions that directly address racial inequity, but their staff and boards are not as diverse as they should be given those missions.

The most interesting statement our leaders made about equity and inclusion is that it is not something you can address once and for all. It is something that you must tackle in good faith, and then address again from a different angle. Our observation is that the initiative often starts with top leadership and is then passed to other employees who have a particular interest in the issue.

Share Our Strength, which is focused on ending childhood hunger in the United States, identifies about 20 percent of its staff as being of color, as compared with 38 percent in the population as a whole.[4] Billy Shore, founder and CEO, is committed to changing this. He says, "We just had a meeting about how we are not where we want to be. ... We asked and answered questions to determine how many privileges we had and to gauge people's reactions. It is something we are working on."

Some of our interviewees' organizations include racial equity as part of their mission. Even in these organizations,

---

4   U.S. Census 2010.

the leaders are asking how they can do more. Amy Houston affirms that this is at the heart of the Robin Hood Foundation's mission, and acknowledges, "There is so much more we can do to be better at this." She is contemplating whether Robin Hood should fund advocacy as well as the work on the ground.

Some of our interviewees are experts in addressing this challenge. Nonet Sykes is director of race equity and inclusion at the Annie E. Casey Foundation, which works to build a brighter future for children, families and communities. Recently, the foundation decided to make racial equity one of its explicit priorities. Sykes says, "I see us applying our racial equity and inclusion knowledge, tools and strategies more precisely to our work over the next few years, with much better understanding and articulation of root causes. We will also be implementing an equity scorecard. That will allow us to trace and measure our progress towards operationalizing the foundation's commitment to equity and inclusion across five core areas: strategy, governance, operations, human resources and investments."

E. Invest Time In Managing Your Board

If you learn one thing from this book, let it be this. Strong boards, well-managed, make everything else easier, from outreach and fund-raising to service delivery and scaling. If you are the CEO of an organization or want to be one, learn how to build a strong board and make it a top priority.

Teresa Younger, CEO of the Ms. Foundation for Women, says, "CEOs rarely recognize that a board takes true board management and time." In the crush of daily responsibilities, it is easy to get pulled away from this labor-intensive activity.

Bob Forrester, CEO of Newman's Own Foundation, says, "At the end of the day, I want a board with competency and empathy, that can distinguish its role from that of management, but still make management appropriately accountable. That's the absolute key to a mature, effective, always relevant nonprofit."

Kevin McMahon of the Pittsburgh Cultural Trust says, "I would say the most important thing about our ability to maintain our leadership position in the region as a leading institution is because of the nature of our board."

We will not focus here on developing your board, although we have led many workshops on the subject. We do recommend a few simple steps to ensure that your board is the best it can possibly be.

Assess the composition of your board. Do you have enough people who have competence in the fields related to your mission? Do you have enough people with operational expertise, like accounting, marketing and law? Do you have enough people with a certain degree of wealth, however you define wealth in your community?

The next step is to decide what kinds of board members you need. If you were considering restricting your candidates to the wealthy, please go back to the drawing board. Your organization deserves nothing less than a board that has both commitment to your cause and the philanthropic capacity to support it.

Then identify people in your community or service area you would like to have on your board. Aim high. There are many ways to do this, such as identifying links with current board members, conducting research and using paid online services. Once you know the people you want, the work of finding connections to them begins. We have a number of tools we use for this, but you can start by simply ramping up your networking with community leaders you already know.

Get to know potential candidates before you ask them to join your board. You also want them to get to know your organization. Inviting them to events and giving them tours of your facility are great ways to do this. Once they agree to join, give them a personalized orientation and have an experienced board member buddy with them for the first year.

Then you are on the way to building the board of your dreams!

CHAPTER 6

Thomas Dente
President and CEO, Humentum

As president and CEO of Humentum, Tom Dente is responsible for developing and executing the organization's strategy and ensuring its overall performance as Humentum evolves to support the needs of its members, clients, customers and partners in a changing sector. Before the merger of InsideNGO with LINGOs and Mango to create Humentum, he had been serving as InsideNGO's president and CEO since early 2016. He joined InsideNGO in January 2011 as chief operating officer.

Previously, Dente was a partner at both Bain & Company and A.T. Kearney, two global management consulting firms, where he worked with senior leaders on strategy development, organizational effectiveness and performance improvement in a career of more than two decades as a management consultant. During his consulting career, he worked with both nonprofit and commercial organizations across North America, Europe and Asia. He has also worked with the Criterion Institute, and began his career in the strategy practice of Price Waterhouse.

Dente serves on the board of directors for InterAction, the alliance of U.S.-based NGOs, as well as the board of directors for PM4NGOs, a global nonprofit focusing on project management in the development sector. He has also served on the C-suite advisory committee of Independent Sector and participated in the Transnational NGO Initiative at the Maxwell School at Syracuse University.

He graduated in economics from Dartmouth College and earned an M.B.A. in finance and marketing from Columbia University's Graduate Business School. He lives with his family in New Rochelle, New York.

Humentum

Humentum is a global membership association of 330 nongovernmental organizations, partners and sector experts in the international development and humanitarian community working together to build organizational and operational capacity. Its mission is to inspire and achieve operational excellence for those organizations working for positive social impact.

Humentum provides training and learning opportunities, peer-to-peer exchange, consulting and recruiting services, and links to industry partners to help organizations operating in the global development sector build their operational and management capacity.

Founded in July 2017, when three successful organizations—InsideNGO, LINGOs and Mango—merged, Humentum has offices in Washington, D.C., and Oxford, England, as well as regional hubs in Africa and Latin America, with experts based in a range of countries around the world. Humentum delivers nearly 400 learning events a year, both face-to-face and online, around the world. Examples include *Fighting Fraud in NGOs* and *Getting the Financial Basics Right.*

Derived from the words "human" and "momentum," the name Humentum captures the importance that people and human capacity play in advancing development and moving social change forward.

Thomas Dente

Thus far, what have been the worst and best events in your life, and what did those experiences teach you?

The best thing that ever happened to me was when I was named CEO of my organization. I'd worked with the organization for five years, so for me it was very exciting, because of the confidence the board and the team placed in me. While it's the best thing that happened to me, at the same time, I was thinking, "Now I really have to execute. What can I deliver? How do I live up to this trust? This is serious now."

For our organization, there are so many nice moments when we're working with members around the world, and I think of their generosity in supporting us and participating with us. It's inspiring. I think it's our hidden strength and that it makes us feel like we can do a lot of things.

If tragedy struck and you couldn't do this kind of work going forward, what's the single most important piece of advice you would have for the next person to try to step into those shoes?

One would be to take the work seriously, but don't take yourself seriously. I'd also say it's not about the answer. It's about how you get to the answer, and being inclusive all the way through that journey. Bring your team, board and communities along. People always talk about communication, but I don't think that's the most important thing. It needs to be more. It's really re-recruiting. You're always re-recruiting people to the mission, to the value that they provide, and to the roles across all levels.

What is your definition of happiness?

I think it's doing something challenging that you can accomplish. It's being in a classic state of flow, where you lose a sense of time, and what you're doing becomes what you are. That's happiness for me. It's different from comfort. I think we often confuse comfort with happiness, but happiness is different. It's taking on meaningful challenges that stretch you and force you to learn. It's the experience of being in that moment, when you're pushing yourself.

What is the most important thing you tell young people who are thinking about making careers in the nonprofit sector?

Have a high tolerance for ambiguity. This sector is constantly reinventing itself in a very positive way, because evidence, data and the nature of problems continue to evolve. When I was younger, a supervisor of mine said, "The most important thing I look for when hiring is people who are flexible." People thinking about making careers in this sector need to be comfortable with flexibility and willing to experiment. Take a growth mindset, not a fixed mindset, and come into this with that perspective. You'll learn a tremendous amount, but you have to be willing to experiment, take risks and fail. Know that there is never one way or one answer; nothing is ever fully solved, and you never get to the bottom of your list.

Last year, I ran my 100th marathon in Havana, and what I've learned from marathons is that you have to set ambitious goals, but it's OK to fail. I haven't finished all of my races. Something always goes wrong in every race. You break your sunglasses, you miss three water stops, it's too hot, too hilly, too rainy. That's totally normal.

The exciting part is that with that mindset, you're able to work with like-minded people who are always testing the status quo and challenging conventional wisdom. That's a tremendous environment to be a part of, especially in the earlier stages of your career. When you're in school, you can't make mistakes because of your grades, tests and numbers. But in your career, you have to take risks. You won't grow if you don't push yourself out there enough to be uncomfortable and potentially fail.

What new opportunities do you see for your organization in the next five years?

If we look ahead in our sector, it's a period of unprecedented change, ranging from funding to attracting talent to delivering our missions. There's never been a time for such innovation and creativity, and I think that's what we'll see in the next 5 or 10 years. There'll be a tremendous amount of creativity in terms of how we do our work, and how we partner and collaborate. It's very exciting, and I think other sectors will look to the nonprofit sector and see there's a lot of innovation going on here, and they'll want to borrow from us.

I see us supporting NGOs globally in many new ways. I think we have to make our learning and our insights more available to people who have never traveled to Nairobi, or Bangkok, or Washington, or London—the places where we have in-person events. We'll spend a lot of time thinking about how to use technology to make e-learning and learning available to those who need it the most around the world. That will be a big change for us in the future, and if we do it well, we'll be able to reach more people who need the insight from their peers in learning. I think that would make more of a difference.

If you could invite five living people to a meeting to have a discussion that would change how the nonprofit sector evolved over the next five years, who would you invite to that conversation, and what would you talk about?

Bill Gates would be good to speak with, given his resources and funding. He's an innovator in the field, so having him there would be terrific. Hillary Clinton would be a good person to have, because of the role of the government in these issues. It would be helpful to have that perspective from someone who understands government but isn't part of it right now. I'd want people from post-conflict situations and people who have benefited from some of the programs that our members have provided. I'd also want to have a technologist there, who could help us think more clearly in terms of staying connected and delivering differently. Lastly, I'd want a thought-provoking person to challenge the sector and ask, "What more can be done?" I think a critic or skeptic would be helpful, so that we shape the sector of the future, not just replicate what we've done in the past.

I'd ask what we would do differently if we had the mindset that the nonprofit sector would be out of business in 5 or 10 years. Obviously, many problems have a longer duration than that, but I think the forcing mechanism is to say that it's not about our institutions, coalitions or alliances. It's about the change we're trying to make. Can we do that differently by taking off some restraints? It would force a series of conversations about what the big bets are. If we were to focus on five or six things, and get those five or six things right, what would those be, and how would they spill over to other areas? I think a little bit of time pressure and focus could really push that conversation along.

One last thing I'd ask is: How do we collaborate and truly partner across other sectors, like the commercial and government sectors, so that we have sustainability? Governments can provide sustainability by putting policies into place. Markets can bring sustainability by providing economic support for people and helping them to be pro-active economic actors in their own communities.

What surprised you about working in the nonprofit sector?

I was surprised by the incredible passion, enthusiasm and excitement that people bring to their work every day. Whether they're a small community nonprofit or an international NGO, these are people hoping to solve some of the hardest problems. That, to me, was incredibly motivating, because you're with people who truly want to make a difference, and they bring that every single day.

What is one thing you would tell your colleagues who are leading grant-making foundations?

As you're making grants and supporting organizations, please make sure there are appropriate resources for the organizations, so that they not only deliver their programs, but become the organizations they need to be. Delivering impact or results takes investment in what is traditionally called overhead or indirect cost. Let's move away from those artificial labels and just talk about what are the true costs of getting the results we want. Let's fund full cost where we can, so we achieve the results we desire. Let's not be guided by dated, old-fashioned accounting metrics, but by impact. There are great organizations doing great work, so let's fund them appropriately.

CHAPTER 7

Bob Giannino

Chief Executive Officer, uAspire

Since 2005, Bob Giannino has served as the chief executive officer of uAspire. In his time, he has overseen the growth of uAspire from a small, local organization serving 1,000 young people in Boston to a national, award-winning organization reaching more than 25 states and 300,000 students each year. Prior to joining uAspire, he served in numerous roles at Jumpstart for Young Children, including serving on the

National Management Team, most recently as vice president of business development and government relations.

Giannino is on the faculty of the Institute for Nonprofit Practice and serves on numerous boards, including Idealist. org, the world's largest nonprofit Internet job site, Root Cause and Harvard's Phillips Brooks House Association, as well as the Advisory Boards of Excel Academy Charter Schools and Noonan Scholars. In 2015, he was awarded the prestigious Barr Fellowship for his "outstanding contribution to the Boston community and potential to drive positive change for years to come." Over the years, he has also been recognized by New Profit, Freedom House, the Boston Business Journal, the Harvard Club of Boston and the Association of Independent Colleges and Universities.

As the first in his family to attend college, a product of the Somerville (MA) Public Schools, and a graduate of Harvard College, Bob knows the vital role that strong financial guidance and minimizing debt plays in ensuring a strong economic future. Bob resides in Dorchester, Massachusetts, and his son, Connor, is a second-year member of the City Year Corps.

uAspire

uAspire is a national leader in providing college affordability services to young people, families and college access and success practitioners. Through local operations in Massachusetts (in Boston, Lawrence, Fall River, Somerville, Malden and Cambridge) and the San Francisco Bay Area (in San Francisco, Oakland and Hayward), training partnerships reaching more than 25 states, and a national virtual advising effort, uAspire will touch the lives of more than 300,000 young people in 2017. uAspire has been featured in numerous media outlets for its expertise on issues of college affordability, including NPR, *Time* magazine, *The New York Times*, *The Boston Globe*, *HuffPost*, *The Chronicle of Higher Education* and *National Journal*. Since 2010, uAspire has received the Organization of Excellence Award by the National College Access Network, was named a Social Innovator by the Social Innovation Forum, was recognized by Opportunity Knocks as one of the nation's "Best Nonprofits to Work For" and the Boston Foundation for "exceptional nonprofit leadership," and was recipient of Year Up's Urban Empowerment Award.

Bob Giannino

At what point in your life did you realize you wanted to make a career in the nonprofit sector, and what was it that made you decide this?

I was very involved in the nonprofit sector in college. I graduated and decided to go into the corporate world, so I worked in sales for Procter & Gamble. I learned a lot about cultivating and developing people to market and sell, but at the end of the day, I did not feel good about it.

About two years into my time in the private sector, I decided that I wasn't having my soul satisfied with the work that I did every day. My mind was being challenged, and I was doing good work that was helping me learn and develop and grow. But it was toward an end that felt much more connected to driving profit and shareholder return than changing communities.

Could you tell me a story about a time when you were most proud to be a part of this sector?

It would have to be in the months after 9/11. I was working in early childhood literacy and was connected to a national service movement. I wasn't working on an issue related to diversity and tolerance. I felt very much a part of the fabric of the social world. I was part of the response to what happened in New York and places where events like 9/11 had occurred.

We were focused on how our sector could play a role in pushing back against anti-Muslim sentiment. We wanted to ensure the pendulum didn't swing so far that it left people out of discussions. Every part of the sector had a role in maintaining true American ideals. Even our work at Jumpstart became about finding our role as an early childhood literacy organization. We wanted to ensure that our communities were safe and that our citizens were protected and heard.

Thus far, what have been the worst and best events in your life, and what did those experiences teach you?

The worst thing is not a moment in time. I am experiencing it and learning from it right now. My parents were high school dropouts, and I am the first in my family to have gone to college. We were a working-class family with very few resources. I grew up in an environment that was not privileged, and I had the opportunity to go to a great college that put me on the path to success. Somehow, along the way, I lost sight of where I came from. The organization I lead is overall very diverse, but at the leadership level, it's very white.

I have a certain amount of disappointment in myself for having lost sight of where I came from. I needed others to point it out to me, and it has created a level of humility that has launched me into action. My organization and I have owned it, and we are putting a significant amount of effort toward changing it and doing it differently. I believe that I will be a better leader and the organization will be better because of this change.

The best thing that happened to me was when my son graduated from college and decided to join City Year as his first job. I could point out a dozen things that have happened, but I'm not sure they were the result of my leadership.

The reason I'm pointing out this personal example is because I was thinking about my son when I left P&G. Would I be proud talking to him about leading a purposeful life? I have not deliberately tried to influence him in any direction at any point in his life. I never had a conversation with him about making a career in the nonprofit sector.

The lesson I learned is that your actions and the tone you set with all the different people around you matter. People are paying attention, even when you are not trying to make them pay attention. Kids are watching what we say, what we do, and how authentic we are. They are going to do something as a result of watching and listening. If we say harsh things or are making choices based on protecting our own self-interest, then that is the society we will continue to have.

If tragedy struck, and you couldn't do this kind of work going forward as of tomorrow, what's the single most important piece of advice you have for the next person to try to step into your shoes?

Create some structure around dialogue, listening and understanding what's going on with the tone and tenor of your organization. As an organization grows, we get farther and farther from what people are feeling and thinking on a daily basis. It gets harder, structurally and interpersonally, for senior executives to really know what's going on. Most of us act when we know things aren't right, but over the years, going from a staff of five to 80, you lose touch with what people need and want in their work life. So if you don't know, you don't act.

Layers of organization get in the way of knowing and acting. I would say to build structures where you break down that bureaucracy. It could be something interpersonal, such as monthly coffees with the CEO, or surveys and interviews. There are many ways to create listening and responsiveness, and it has to be there for your organization to be healthy.

We have created an internal cross-functional team focused on equity and representation. We are identifying opportunities for our leaders to have deep, significant training in inclusion and equity. Our president and I are regularly meeting with that team to make it a leadership issue. I am doing much more frequent meetings with different members of our organization to engage everyone.

What is your definition of happiness?

I'm happiest when my life is in balance. I want to be doing good work toward an end. I care about the means and the ends. I also want a fulfilling personal life, so I am equally excited and disappointed about going to work on Monday.

What is the most important thing you tell young people who are thinking about making careers in the nonprofit sector?

I hear from a lot of younger people that they want to do something, and they have this assumption that since they thought of it, nobody else has. I ask them, "Do you know this organization? Have you talked to this person?" Don't assume that what you want to do in the world is not already being done.

I'd also tell them to maintain their balance. Sustainability in community work requires a good work-life balance. I cannot tell you how many 30-somethings have done this work for five to seven years and are already burnt out. They dive in, and that may not sustain over time. We need people who are committed to this work and can sustain themselves over this trajectory for decades.

What new opportunities do you see for your organization in the next five years?

Making access to higher education more affordable is more important than ever before. There are people being left behind in our country who are not on the opportunity bus, and they need to be. I'm speaking about rural folks and folks who live in former manufacturing areas. Jobs they lost will not be available to them, and we are very much a part of the solution moving forward.

If you could invite five living people to a meeting to have a discussion that would change how the nonprofit sector evolved over the next five years, who would you invite to that conversation, and what would you talk about?

I would invite Marian Wright Edelman [of the Children's Defense Fund], Dorothy Stoneman [of YouthBuild USA], Darell Hammond [founder of KaBOOM!], Darren Walker [of the Ford Foundation] and former first lady Michelle Obama. The agenda would be how to catalyze impact in the 21st century. How do we think about the spread and scale of the need that exists in our country? How do we think differently about putting a dent in the need that exists on so many fronts, like hunger, health disparities and educational attainment? I picked those people because they have all done that work or have the kind of voice that could move the needle.

If there were one thing you could say to your colleagues who are leading grant-making foundations, what would it be?

Give as much attention to the health and well-being of the organizations you are investing in as you do the programs they deliver. There has been a good conversation about impact and outcomes, but we have not paid enough attention to making sure that organizations are sustainable and healthy enough to continue to deliver those outcomes over a long period of time.

CHAPTER 8

Paula Kerger
President and CEO, PBS

Paula Kerger is president and CEO of PBS, the nation's largest noncommercial media organization, with nearly 350 member stations. Since her arrival in 2006, Kerger has made particularly strong commitments to the arts, news and public affairs, high-quality educational content for children and the classroom, diversity and the use of new digital platforms to bring public media into the lives of all Americans.

Kerger is also president of the PBS Foundation, an independent organization that raises private sector funding for PBS, and has become a significant source of revenue for new projects at PBS.

Kerger received her bachelor's degree from the University of Baltimore, where she serves on the Merrick School of Business Dean's Advisory Council. She has received honorary doctorates from Washington University in St. Louis, Grand Valley State University and Allegheny College. She is a director of the International Academy of Television Arts and Sciences and chair of the Board of the Smithsonian Institution's National Museum of Natural History.

PBS

PBS is a private, nonprofit corporation, founded in 1969, whose members are the United States' public TV stations—noncommercial, educational licensees that operate 350 PBS member stations and serve all 50 states, Puerto Rico, U.S. Virgin Islands, Guam and American Samoa.

Each month, PBS reaches nearly 100 million people through television and nearly 28 million people online, inviting them to experience the worlds of science, history, nature and public affairs; to hear diverse viewpoints; and to take front-row seats to world-class drama and performances. PBS' broad array of programs has been consistently honored with the industry's most coveted awards.

Teachers of children from pre-K through 12th grade turn to PBS for digital content and services that help bring classroom lessons to life. Decades of research confirm that

PBS' premier children's media service, PBS KIDS, helps children build critical literacy, math and social-emotional skills, enabling them to find success in school and life. Delivered through member stations, PBS KIDS offers high-quality educational content on TV—including a new 24/7 channel, online at pbskids.org, via an array of mobile apps and in communities across the United States. Year after year, PBS and its member stations are rated No. 1 in public trust among nationally known institutions.

Paula Kerger

How would you describe PBS' role in creating positive social change?

For nearly 50 years, PBS has focused on fulfilling our founding mission—to educate, entertain and inspire the American public. Unlike commercial media, we exist to serve, not sell to, our audiences. At a time when 1 in 5 households do not have cable or satellite and 16 percent lack access to broadband, public television is the only window that many Americans have to the broader world. No matter where they live, and no matter their economic means, everyone should have access to content that helps them lead meaningful and engaged lives.

Public television is available to nearly every single household in the United States through nearly 350 local member stations, and we leverage our broad reach to present content that often cannot be found anywhere else on television, including in-depth journalism, arts and culture, and science and natural history programming.

At the heart of our work is education, and we have a relentless commitment to preparing the next generation for the opportunities and challenges ahead. PBS KIDS reaches more children ages 2 to 5, more kids in low-income homes and more moms with young children than any other children's TV network. Every program we put on air and online is geared toward learning and discovery. We present curriculum-based content that is proven to move the needle in children's learning, and we partner with schools and teachers to extend the impact of our work into the classroom.

Our greatest differentiator is the fact that public television has a national reach with a community presence. In fact, public television stations and radio stations are among the last locally owned and operated broadcasters. Each station tailors its programming and services to meet the unique needs of the community.

Through our on-the-ground presence, public television brings communities together for civil discourse, at a time when it is so desperately needed. Let me give you an example. In the fall of 2017, we presented Ken Burns' and Lynn Novick's *The Vietnam War*, an in-depth, holistic look at the nation-defining event as never before seen on television. In conjunction with the film, local stations hosted community events, convened roundtable forums and helped people share their stories from the war.

Simply put, I believe that public television plays an incredibly important role in supporting the health and vibrancy of our country.

The New York Times has reported that "the widening political divergence between cities and small-town America reflects a growing alienation between the two groups, and a sense—perhaps accurate—that their fates are not connected." What role could the nonprofit sector play to help the two groups find greater common ground?

The nonprofit sector has an important role to play in bridging those divides. Over the past two decades, there has been a significant erosion of the public's trust in national institutions. People are yearning to connect with organizations that they trust, organizations that are focused on meeting the needs of their families and their communities. Speaking for PBS, I can tell you that we are proud that Americans' trust in public television remains extremely high. PBS is not only the most trusted media institution, but year after year, we are rated the most trusted among nationally known institutions. That trust cuts across geographic, political and socio-economic lines.

In part, we attribute this to our constant focus on high-quality content. When we take on a new project or program, the question is not: How will it make us money? The question is: How will it help the people who watch our content? Take our news and public affairs, for example. Our viewers appreciate that we aren't interested in getting a sensational soundbite; rather, we are interested in getting at the truth. We give time and oxygen to the pressing issues of our time, and we focus on presenting information without hyperbole and without spin.

Equally important to the content that we put on air is the fact that public television is inherently local. We aren't some faraway media network; we are a media system that is in your backyard focusing on the issues that matter to your community. There are lessons here for organizations in any industry. If the public believes that you have a vested interest in their community, then that in turn generates an enormous amount of trust and goodwill among the people you serve.

At what point in your life did you realize you wanted to make a career in the nonprofit sector, and what was it that made you decide this?

I come from a family that was deeply involved in community service, which instilled in me at a young age the importance of giving back and serving a purpose greater than myself. However, I did not start my career with service in mind. I left college with a business degree, and I assumed I'd end up working for a corporation. But as fate would have it, I landed a job at UNICEF. It was there that I developed a passion for nonprofit work, which led to a job with International House, then the Metropolitan Opera, and eventually, I ended up at Channel 13 WNET, the PBS station in New York.

Could you tell me a story about a time when you were most proud to be a part of this sector?

It's hard to point to one singular moment. I am proud each and every day when I see how public television is delivering on our mission. Whether it's a child who sees the world open up to them through PBS KIDS characters on the screen, a young adult who is drawn to the stage after watching a theatrical performance on TV, or a family living in a rural area that connects to the outside world through their local station, there are countless stories of people whose lives have been enriched and enhanced by public television.

What was the worst thing that ever happened to you, and what did you learn from it?

Given the breadth and depth of content that PBS presents each year, we will occasionally air a program that inadvertently generates controversy among a subset of our viewing population. I can think of one example that was particularly challenging. Several years ago, we presented a program that—despite receiving widespread acclaim—did not sit well with one community. On one hand, we had an artist who was concerned that we stand by his work, and on the other, we had various community groups demanding that we pull the film from our schedule. PBS was caught in the middle. I learned a lot of lessons from that experience, but most of all, it reinforced the importance of relationships. To navigate through the complexity of the situation and to reach a solution that would work for all parties, I developed relationships with organizations that I hadn't previously encountered in my day-to-day work. In doing so, I developed more direct and candid lines of communication with the organizers behind the protest. No matter the crisis or situation, communication is extremely important. I also learned that the only way to manage through a crisis is to address it head on and drive toward some kind of resolution; Otherwise, it never really disappears, and you risk taking a permanent hit to your reputation and credibility.

If tragedy struck and you couldn't do this kind of work going forward as of tomorrow, what's the single most important piece of advice you have for the next person to try to step into your shoes?

I am a firm believer in the importance of succession planning and having leaders in place who are prepared to take the helm. At PBS, we spend a lot of time on succession planning for key positions across the organization.

As for the advice I would give to someone stepping into my shoes, I would say that you need to be able to listen well, pull together information, consider different points of view, and most important, you must be decisive. As CEO, you have to remember that you are the decision maker, and the buck stops with you. It's also important to remember that we are all going to make mistakes, and when we do make a mistake, the key is to learn from that mistake and immediately pivot. You cannot let mistakes paralyze you, because if you fail to move forward, the organization will stall.

How has social media changed your business model?

Social media has enhanced our ability to engage with audiences in new and different ways. For one, it has enabled us to connect with viewers who may not have historically watched public television. When *Downton Abbey* started becoming a hit, we saw an explosion of activity online and across platforms, especially among younger audiences. There were .gifs and memes and spoof videos, and while PBS helped to feed the conversation, much of the activity was organic and driven by the people who had fallen in love with the show.

Social media has also helped us to create a more engaging experience with our content. We already do this at the local level through screenings and community conversations; social media is a natural extension of those conversations. Let me give you an example. Last fall, PBS and stations presented *Hamilton's America*, a behind-the-scenes look at the smash hit musical. On the day of the premiere, we presented the documentary on multiple platforms, including Facebook Live. There were 1.1 million views on Facebook on the first day alone, making it the No. 1-ranked social program of the night. Platforms such as these provide us with a new way to invite audiences into the conversation.

What is your definition of happiness?

Professionally, I am happiest when I know that I'm contributing to work that is making a meaningful difference in people's lives. Personally, I have a great affinity for the arts, and I'm especially delighted when I have the opportunity to enjoy musical theater and dance.

What is the most important thing you tell young people who are thinking about making careers in the nonprofit sector?

The nonprofit sector is not only a place to make your mark on the world; it's also a great place to make a career. The advice I would give to young people considering working for a nonprofit is no different from the advice I would give to anyone else—no matter your path, leave yourself open to possibility. When I graduated from college, I couldn't have told you that I would end up where I am today. I've been fulfilled throughout my career because I've been willing to embrace opportunity when it comes my way. The most interesting opportunities I've come across were usually the ones I would have never even considered. As human beings, we are often stymied by inertia, and we tend to stay on a path that's comfortable. But sometimes, to do something that's exhilarating, you have to do something that's a little bit terrifying.

What new opportunities do you see for your organization in the next five years?

PBS operates in one of the most dynamic and rapidly evolving industries, and for us, an ongoing challenge is how we continue to meet consumers where, when and how they consume content. In recent years, PBS and local stations have greatly expanded the distribution of our programming across online and digital platforms, and we will continue to do so as we move into the future. At the same time, we remain deeply committed to ensuring that all Americans have access to public television through over-the-air broadcast, which is especially important to rural and underserved areas that would be cut off from the outside world were it not for their local station.

We also see a tremendous opportunity in the education space. PBS has a nearly 50-year legacy of educational programming that began with *Mister Rogers' Neighborhood*. That legacy carries through today in programs such as *Daniel Tiger's Neighborhood* and *Wild Kratts*. There is no issue of greater import to our nation's future than the education of our children. This year, we doubled down on our efforts by launching a 24/7 PBS KIDS broadcast and live stream, available to families at every hour of every day. We are also expanding our services in the classroom, by connecting teachers to digital resources and peer networks, which is really the next frontier of our education work.

On the programmatic side, we continue to wrestle with the issue of the arts. PBS is the only place where many Americans can experience the extraordinary theater, dance and music that are the legacy of this country. As I've traveled extensively in my job, I've seen amazing performances in communities across the country. Our challenge is to figure out how we capture that art and bring it to a national audience, and in particular, how we continue to give kids exposure to things that might spark their passion.

We are in the midst of a national conversation about race and racial equity. What is your organization doing, both internally and externally, to address racial inequity?

The country's increasing diversity is tremendously important to PBS, as we look at people in front of and behind the camera. We have a number of formal programs that we've implemented within PBS and across the system to support emerging leaders who come from different backgrounds and bring new perspectives.

Public television has a long legacy of supporting diverse filmmakers, and we are equally committed to presenting programs that shine a light on the importance of diversity to our nation's history. As one example, this fall we will present Raoul Peck's documentary *I Am Not Your Negro*, which explores race relations in America through the perspective of the writer James Baldwin.

If there were one thing you could say to your colleagues who are leading grant-making foundations, what would it be?

I would encourage them to be a partner to the organizations they fund. At the end of the day, grantors and grantees want the same thing: to make an impact. When the organization writing the check views their role as a partner to the organization they are funding, it usually results in the best possible outcome.

I would also recommend that they give the grantee the flexibility to experiment and the permission to fail. At PBS, we occasionally take on projects that do not yield the outcome we'd anticipated, but often that is when we discover the biggest and most promising ideas.

CHAPTER 9

Be Crystal Clear About Your Goal, and Articulate It Persuasively

Once you have sharpened your skills and ensured that your house is in order, you are ready to frame your goal in a way that resonates with the largest possible number of people. This may seem an obvious step, but in our experience, this is something many nonprofits do not spend enough time on. Nor do they test their message with enough people before adopting it.

We identified the following components of this principle from our interviews and our many years of working for and with nonprofits.

A. Define the Outcome Specifically

This idea will not surprise anyone who has worked in the nonprofit sector in the past 15 years. The trend toward results, or outcomes-based, planning and evaluation is well established.

Muhammed Chaudhry is executive director of the Silicon Valley Education Foundation (SVEF), which is "dedicated to putting all students on track for college and careers, focusing on the critical areas of science, technology, engineering and math (STEM)."[5] Chaudhry advises, "Don't try to do it all. Maintain absolute focus. Stay true to the core mission to build up. We wanted to do much more, to create programs for all of the STEM fields. Our chairman said, pick one! So we picked math." In 2015, the nonprofit education research organization WestEd deemed SVEF's signature program, ElevateMath!, twice as effective as similar programs in preparing students to study algebra the following year. This improvement was achieved with only 19 days of summer instruction.

Chaudhry adds, "Before you seek funding, truly seek agreement on how the dial will be moved, on the measurement, then the solution. Tell me the dial you want to move. What number, if moved, would impact the rest? For me, it's the number of students that graduate from high school having completed the courses required for college."

Chaudhry is clear about the outcome he seeks, and he can measure it relatively easily. The University of California system has a list of courses it requires students to complete before they can even apply to a UC school. On that list are three math courses: elementary algebra, geometry and intermediate algebra.

---

5   Silicon Valley Education Foundation, "About Us." http://svefoundation. org/pages/about-us/ (accessed August 2, 2017).

Some outcomes are much harder to measure. In our strategic planning work, people often ask us if all the goals in a plan need to be quantitative. The answer is no—but the results do have to be measurable. We were working recently with an organization that teaches ethics to graduate students. This organization was wrestling with how to measure the outcomes of its programs. It is clearly impossible to know with certainty whether the alumni will make more ethical decisions than they would have had they not taken the program.

The solution is surveying the students and the alumni about their thoughts and actions, preferably over time, i.e. before they start the program, after they finish the program and at intervals afterwards. Although this self-reporting is not ideal, it is really the only way to measure the outcome of the program.

Amy Houston of the Robin Hood Foundation agrees with Chaudhry. She has worked on both the grant-seeking and grant-making sides of the equation. She puts it this way. "People with clear vision win the game. Have confidence in and clarity about the product you are delivering. Do one thing incredibly well, versus trying to do a little bit of everything."

We believe the nonprofit world has become overly preoccupied with trying to measure results, but the trend shows no sign of abating. Asking small nonprofits to measure outcomes can backfire, unless the funder is going to provide the funding to do the evaluation, because the nonprofits don't think they have the resources both to deliver their programs and to evaluate them. Robert M. Penna, PhD, in his book about outcomes, begs to differ.[6] He makes the case that designing programs with evaluation in mind makes it much easier to measure the programs' effectiveness. He also argues, persuasively, that if you don't know which of your programs is working better than the others, you won't know which ones to expand if you get a windfall or which to cut if you have to reduce your budget.

B. Frame the Issue Appropriately

Making the case for pursuing your goal is a critical element of reaching it. Another way of expressing this idea is that you have to be able to tell people why your organization exists, in a concise, powerful way. We call that statement your mission statement, and it should not change very often.

Over time, however, organizations' missions do change. Bill Ulfelder, New York executive director of the Nature Conservancy, in discussing the opportunities he sees for the Conservancy over the next five years, reflected on a subtle but important change in the way the Conservancy now talks about its ultimate goal. "No. 1 is changing the Nature Conservancy's mission from being strictly nature- or biodiversity-focused to conserving the lands and waters on which all life depends," he explains. "It's more of a statement about the well-being of humanity."

The Conservancy is broadening its mission because the future of the planet depends on it. It is also changing its mission because its leadership recognizes that more people can

6   *The Nonprofit Outcomes Toolbox: A Complete Guide to Program Effectiveness, Performance Measurement, and Results*, Robert M. Penna, PhD, Hoboken: John Wiley & Sons, Inc., 2011.

resonate with the idea of conserving the lands and waters on which all life depends.

Dan Gross, president of the Brady Campaign to Prevent Gun Violence and one of our former clients, has a background in advertising. Before he came to the Brady Center in 2011, he co-founded and ran an organization called PAX, focused on youth violence prevention. Gross says, "The organization was successful because we approached it the right way, and it tied into my genuine passion for marketing, communications and insight. It filled a vital role in addressing the gun violence purely as the public health and safety issue that it is, while steering completely clear of politics."

Gross persuasively argues that nonprofits have been slow to learn from the growing corporate focus on social science as a tool to help organizations communicate their missions more powerfully. He was a major driver in shifting the focus of the debate around gun control.

We interviewed Sally Osberg, CEO of the Skoll Foundation. The foundation "drives large-scale change by investing in, connecting and celebrating social entrepreneurs and the innovators who help them solve the world's most pressing problems."[7] Osberg says, "I think one of the dimensions of our impact has been the work we do in media and communications, which is inspired by Jeff Skoll's belief in the power of a story well-told. We want to shine a light on the most important issues in the world and their solutions." Skoll has partnerships with PBS, Sundance, the BBC

7   Skoll Foundation, home page. http://skoll.org/ (accessed August 6, 2017).

and *The Guardian*—entities which are serious about telling the story well.

C. Ensure Your Solution Can Be Enlarged With Quality

The nonprofit sector is currently obsessed with taking solutions to social problems to scale. This has grown out of the work of social entrepreneurs who founded such organizations as Teach for America or Habitat for Humanity. These people were able to scale their organizations far beyond the point most nonprofits can ever aspire to. As Leon Botstein of Bard College says, "The greatest physician in the world is not necessarily the person who reaches the largest number of people. It's the one with the most effective medical intervention that can be replicated, so that if you discover a cure for polio or a major disease, it can be distributed in a way that reaches a mass population."

Amy Houston of the Robin Hood Foundation worries about the challenge of continuing the process of reinvention, of finding the next big idea and scaling it up. She says, "There are far fewer solutions than people like to acknowledge—and very few great solutions. The trick is identifying them, and then scaling them, if they can be scaled."

Houston's remark is worth considering carefully. One of the most worrisome trends in philanthropy is that, in looking for the next big idea, philanthropists may ignore ideas that have already been shown to work. Even worse, they could spend money looking for new ideas when they should spend it on evaluating approaches that are already being piloted.

Larry Kramer of the Hewlett Foundation puts it this way. "Dealing with social problems like poverty, racism, climate change or income inequality is not like developing a new piece of software. Progress is slow not from lack of imagination or willingness to take chances, but because the problems are *hard.*"

One organization working seriously to scale its impact is the Mental Health Association of New York City (MHA-NYC). MHA-NYC addresses mental health needs in New York City and across the nation. Its best-known program is the National Suicide Prevention Lifeline.

Kim Williams, its CEO, says, "I think the greatest opportunity for us is around the advancements in technology. Technology has really opened a new frontier in providing access and support for mental health and also around data collection and reporting, and analytics. I think that there will continue to be opportunities to extend one of our core assets, and to focus on technology-enabled service, to both facilitate access to people and provide them with direct support." MHA-NYC has developed its call center capabilities over many years, which has left it in a good position to take advantage of these changes in technology.

It is important to note that not all important and necessary programs can be successfully amplified and taken to the next level. Ellen LaPointe of Northern California Grantmakers says, "Everything that needs funding does not need to be globally scalable to be deeply important and valuable to the well-being of a community and its people. Scalability is obviously an important thing to consider, but it is not always relevant to something that may be, nevertheless, essential."

D. Raise Seed Funding

Anyone who has raised money, whether for ending hunger globally or fixing up a local park or school, knows it is not easy. Competition for philanthropic dollars is fierce. Of the 1.7 million nonprofits in the United States, about 1 million are public charities that are actively raising funds at any one time. That gives you some sense of the odds.

Regardless of how difficult it is, raise funds you must. Fortunately, today there are more avenues for social purpose funding than there once were. These sources range from traditional philanthropic dollars from individuals, corporations and foundations to businesses that have a social purpose as part of their mission. Warby Parker, the eyeglass manufacturer and distributor, offers one example. Warby Parker helps consumers by selling eyeglasses at a lower cost than traditional manufacturers. The company helps people around the world who need glasses but cannot afford them (about 1 billion people, it estimates) by giving a pair of glasses to one of these people every time they sell a pair to a consumer at full price.

The truth is that most dollars for purposes traditionally funded by charity still come from traditional philanthropic sources. We mention social-purpose businesses because nonprofits should be paying attention to the developments in this space and figuring out how they can eventually tap into this new source of funds.

The source of most philanthropy is individuals, corporations and foundations. It is a little-known fact outside the fund-raising world that as much as 85 percent of those funds come from individuals. Like Willie Sutton, the bank robber who famously said, "I rob banks because that's where the money is," we always tell clients to consider raising funds from individuals first, because "that's where the money is." Of course, there are notable exceptions to this rule, like Susan G. Komen for the Cure, which started by raising corporate dollars and continues to obtain much of its revenue from corporate sources. But Komen is the exception, not the rule.

CHAPTER 10

Michael Capasso

General Director, New York City Opera

Michael Capasso is the general director of the New York City Opera. He has produced, directed and toured opera and musical theater productions in the United States and abroad for over 30 years. In June 2014, along with philanthropist Roy Niederhoffer, he led the successful effort to bring the New York City Opera out of bankruptcy. The revitalized New York City Opera returned to the stage in January 2016, with a celebratory production of *Tosca*. After completing a 2016-17 season of six fully staged productions, the company is once again on solid financial footing.

In 1981, Capasso, along with Diane Martindale, founded New York's Dicapo Opera Theater. Over the 30 years of his leadership, Dicapo Opera Theater presented a diverse program to the New York public.

Capasso has also directed operas at l'Opéra de Montréal; Mallorca Opera; Toledo Opera; Connecticut Opera; New Jersey State Opera; Opera Carolina; and Orlando Opera, among others. He founded the National Lyric Opera in 1991.

In celebration of the 75th anniversary of George Gershwin's *Porgy and Bess*, Capasso mounted a production that began touring in the United States in February 2010. As an author, his writing credits include: a staged adaptation of Dickens' *A Christmas Carol*; *Opera Senza Rancor*; *Puccini's Passion*; a new book and libretto for *La Périchole*; English librettos for *Die Fledermaus* and *The Daughter of the Regiment*; and a concert/lecture series for the New York Historical Society.

In 2016, Capasso was awarded an honorary doctorate from the College of Mount Saint Vincent and the Legends of the Arts award from the Harvard Club. He has received New York City's Ellis Island Medal of Honor, the Licia Albanese-Puccini Foundation's Lifetime Achievement Award, and the Leonardo da Vinci Award for Cultural Achievement from the Italian Heritage and Culture Committee of New York.

New York City Opera

Since its founding in 1943 by Mayor Fiorello LaGuardia as "The People's Opera," New York City Opera has been a critical part of the city's cultural life. During its history, City Opera has launched the careers of dozens of major artists and presented engaging productions of both mainstream and unusual operas alongside commissions and regional premieres. The result is a uniquely American opera company of international stature.

For more than seven decades, City Opera has maintained a distinct identity, adhering to its unique mission: affordable ticket prices, a devotion to American works and English-language performances, the promotion of up-and-coming American singers, and seasons of accessible, vibrant and compelling productions intended to introduce new audiences to the art form. Stars who began their careers at New York City Opera include Plácido Domingo, Beverly Sills, Samuel Ramey and dozens more.

In 1999, New York City Opera founded VOX Contemporary Opera Lab, an annual concert series that offered composers and librettists the opportunity to hear excerpts of their works performed by professional singers and musicians. For decades, City Opera has been committed to introducing opera to the young, bringing the art form to new audiences with educational outreach performances in New York City's public schools.

Now, having returned to the stage, New York City Opera continues its legacy at a new, state-of-the-art home at the Rose Theater at Jazz at Lincoln Center, with revitalized outreach and education programs, and programming designed to welcome and inspire a new generation of City Opera audiences.

Michael Capasso

Who has had the greatest influence on you as a professional?

I don't know that I would be in this business were it not for my fascination with the great Italian tenor Enrico Caruso. His recordings sparked my interest in opera, which led me to read everything I could find about the art form, especially opera in the golden age of the Metropolitan Opera. I read about the impresario Giulio Gatti-Casazza, who was running La Scala in his 30s, when he was brought to the United States to run the Met with Toscanini as music director. In those days, everything, even the signage at the Met, was in Italian. He did an amazing amount of work. He commissioned some of Puccini's greatest operas, but also commissioned works from Deems Taylor and Victor Herbert, which I found fascinating. He commissioned a new American opera every year, because he felt it was important. Unfortunately, that all stopped when Gatti-Casazza retired.

The woman with whom I started the Dicapo Opera Theater, Diane Martindale, really opened a door for me. Before we founded the company, she was my high school music teacher, and she was the one who convinced me that I could do what I'm doing now—that there was a career option for me besides going into the family construction business. She made me believe that if I wanted to run the Met or New York City Opera, I could. She told me that I was smart enough and that my knowledge, and obsession with the art form, could take me far. I wasn't afraid of working, and that started me on the path I'm still on.

Other very influential people include Rudolf Bing, whom I met when I was 17. He had just left the Met; I got an appointment with him and said, "I want to do what you did." He said, "Well, that's great. You need to be lucky, and you need to be in the right place at the right time." He said, "Anybody could have done what I did. I was lucky because I was at the right place at the right time."

The business and artistic plan that we're currently executing is based on the work of City Opera's legendary conductor and general director Julius Rudel. I met with him at his apartment three years ago, shortly after the company had entered bankruptcy. He was near the end of his long life but was still very astute and insightful. He read the plan for reviving City Opera and endorsed it. He liked the balance of the repertoire and thought the idea of presenting a concurrent season of chamber operas at a smaller theater had merit. He gave me a great deal of confidence that we were on the right track, and that helped buoy me through some difficult times and tough negotiations.

Thus far, what have been the worst and best events in your life, and what did those experiences teach you?

The best thing that ever happened to me was deciding that opera would be my career. Loving what I do and knowing there is nothing I'd rather be doing has helped me create opportunities for myself and succeed. It's made me able to stick with it through good times and some really difficult times. I think people shouldn't be in the arts if they can see themselves doing something else. If you can do something else and be happy, do it. Because whatever it is, it's a lot easier than what we choose to do here. But the satisfaction from doing this is second to none for me. It's like a drug; I can't live without it.

What advice would you give to your peers in the nonprofit sector about building an organization or scaling its programs and operations?

Only produce what you're able to produce, and don't get too big too fast. You need to build a solid infrastructure with a group of hardworking and incredibly loyal people. Loyalty is the thing that I treasure the most. My staff and the people around me are incredibly dedicated to the cause and to me personally, and I to them. It's very much a family atmosphere. Gather strong people around you that are like-minded, figure out what it is you do best together and what sets you apart, and then go ahead and do that. Raise the money, and develop an audience. You find more money when there's a niche to be filled. In many ways, there was nothing else like Dicapo in New York. There was the Met and there was the City Opera, but there was no intimate theater offering a full season of professional opera.

I don't know if City Opera will ever return to presenting 160 performances a season, but I do think there's room for the company to grow. We might get to a 75-performance season, which is still far more than regional companies. That would be through a mix of large- and small-scale productions as well as concerts.

I would suggest to anybody that they do whatever they can to stay in front of their public as much as possible, because if you're quiet, people forget. People go where there's activity. I think a mistake made by the last City Opera administration after they left Lincoln Center was that they would program two productions in succession—an opera in October, then November, and then nothing again until March. So, if you couldn't see the productions in October or November, you'd miss half the season. Once the public forgets and goes elsewhere, it's hard to bring them back. I've been very careful to program regular offerings for our audience. In a month when we're not doing a grand opera at Lincoln Center, we're doing a small piece in a 150-seat theater. People are going to know about it, and it will sell out. And it enables us to send an e-blast to 90,000 people, reminding them we're here.

What are your priorities, and what portion of your time do you spend on each of them?

My priorities are to make the company operational, sustainable and relevant again. From an operational point of view, we are currently understaffed because we're being very careful. We have few people who cover many roles. We currently need to grow in the marketing department. We are fully staffed in administration and production.

I focus a great deal on artistic matters, but also on their budgetary practicality, determining what we can do, and how it fits into a well-planned season. Of course, my No. 1 focus is how I'm going to get that season paid for. To get it paid for, I need to fully understand how we're going to do what we propose. If anybody asks me a question about any of our upcoming productions, I can tell them what the principal singers are getting paid, what the scenery's going to cost, what's getting shipped, and where it's coming from. I need to know every single detail about every production. My philosophy about fund-raising is that you need to be able to explain to people where their money is going to go, and why we need the amount we're asking for. I want to know why any given thing costs what it costs so I can give donors confidence to fund it.

We were very fortunate to find the funds to bring the company out of bankruptcy and get back onstage, but we need to continue raising money to sustain the revival. We are still in the process of re-engaging the foundations that contributed a large portion of City Opera's budget in the years before the bankruptcy. We need some of the larger individual donors to come back. That's the push we need right now to get over this next hurdle. I believe we're going to do it; it's just important to execute the plan.

What, if anything, keeps you up at night?

It's always something to do with raising money or spending it. Do we have enough time in the theater? Should we buy projectors or keep renting them? We're spending too much. Why are we spending on this? It follows us everywhere.

What is your definition of happiness, or, what is your philosophy of life?

If you can get up in the morning and be satisfied with where you are and what you have to do that day, then you're a very lucky person. It's all relative. If I have a bad day, at the end of the bad day, I still run the New York City Opera. It's a dream job. My problems are not "We ran out of concrete," or "The steel failed." My problems are artistic. So my philosophy is: Figure out how to keep your life, be satisfied with it, even if you're not satisfied with that day or even a year. When you're in show business, you work the oddest hours and there are no days off. I work hard and my hours are 24 hours a day, but I've managed to position myself so that I'm satisfied with where I am, happy to do what I do, and anxious to move forward.

What is the greatest misconception about you?

Because of my background and my unconventional career path, there are those in the industry who jump to the conclusion that I lack a certain pedigree, and the knowledge that goes along with it. After all, I didn't go to a fancy university or conservatory. I didn't come up through the ranks of big theaters or start as an usher at San Francisco Opera. I did it my way, carving out a career in a theater I founded myself. But from my perspective, the skills I acquired through creating and sustaining a theater for 30 years are what made me able to take on the challenge of turning City Opera around.

Some might think I'm just a contractor who kind of dabbles in the opera business, but the construction business taught me a great deal. I learned how to deal with large crews of people doing multiple tasks in different departments. I learned how to deal with unions and large numbers when it comes to material, equipment, labor and budgeting. Those skills really apply to what I'm doing now. Business is business, and I learned a lot by growing up in that industry. Being able to apply that to the opera puts me in a very strong position.

In 2015, I was working as a construction supervisor for a company that was rebuilding Breezy Point in Queens after Hurricane Sandy. When I read that the City Opera had gone bankrupt, I was horrified. I knew I could do something about it. I found a lawyer to give us a million dollars' worth of pro-bono legal work. I approached Roy Niederhoffer, a City Opera board member who still held out hope for the company's survival. I found a venue and started forging relationships. Most people doubted me, but there were a few people who were on board from the beginning. I managed to succeed.

Anybody in the world could have found a lawyer, come up with a plan, found a patron and put all this together, but nobody else did because everybody thought it was impossible. They didn't have the wherewithal, or maybe just the arrogance, to think that it could be done. Then when it was done, they wondered how it happened.

How would you define the American dream?

If you work hard enough, you can achieve anything you want. You just need to be willing to put in the time. I never changed what I want to do. I've had to change course for a couple of years because I needed to survive, and that was horrible. Others might have given up, but I always knew that somehow I was going to turn it around and get back on track. I didn't know how, and when it presented itself people thought I was stark, raving nuts—including my lawyers.

How important is it to find the right people for your board, and what qualities do you look for? How successful have you been at matching those qualities?

I think the most important thing is the personality match, because the board needs to be engaged with the general director and his/her artistic vision. You've got to find a group of people that like you and the organization, and find what it is that appeals to them so that they are willing to fund it. You can't give them repertoire they hate in a venue they don't like, present it in an uncompelling manner, and then expect them to pay for it. Board members have to be engaged with the company and with the leadership. They have to like and admire the leadership, and be willing to guide and help. I never want to be the smartest person in the room. I want to be surrounded by smart board members and staff. Everybody on my staff is smarter than I am, and I'm not ashamed of it. People in leadership roles have to be able to surround themselves with a cabinet of people they'll listen to.

What is the most important thing you tell young people who are thinking about making careers in the nonprofit sector?

Get experience. Do everything you possibly can, and don't be afraid to jump or fail. You can read books and study with professors, but don't expect to come in and go right to the top. Learn from people who have been through the mill. Get in on the ground floor and soak up information, experiences, productions, and processes. You'll pick things up just being around it all. Don't be afraid to ask questions.

Education is important in this business, but there's nothing greater than experience, especially wide-ranging experience. If you just want to be a CFO, you can do that anywhere. You might learn things about opera, but at the end of the day, you might as well be a CFO for an air-conditioning company. If you want to lead in this industry, you need to be intimately acquainted with all levels of it. The only way to do that is to be involved, watch things develop, and ask questions.

Younger generations aren't taught the realities of the industry, and they come out of school thinking they're going to be a star without doing the work. It's hard to find some-body who is willing to hit the ground. It takes work. One day you're in jeans and work boots, and then the next day, you're in a tuxedo. That's the way it works.

What new opportunities do you see for City Opera in the next five years?

I think in the next five years, City Opera will once again become solidly relevant in the operatic landscape of New York and internationally. I think its budget will grow, and I would like to see it re-establish an endowment so that it's healthy going forward. I'd like the company to be healthy, respected and have critical acclaim. I'd like to regain the trust of the public, because if you have their trust, it gives you a great deal of latitude when it comes to programming. Our last show was fabulous and sold well. It got great reviews and it should have sold out, but it didn't, because people didn't know the title and they don't trust us yet. But in five years, I'd like to be able to program just about anything and have people come because they know it's going to be good.

It might not be something they'll like, but they'll be assured it will have musical and production values that will make it a worthwhile experience. If the public trusts you, then they'll come and donate.

If there were one thing you could say to the world's billionaire philanthropists, what would it be?

Don't ignore us; listen to us. The nonprofit sector is a major part of what fuels this country. We are relevant, and what we do is valid. If they would take a look and let us talk to them, I think they'd be surprised what an enormous impact they could have on the industry, and what an impact the industry has on the national economy. Give us a chance. People think these arts are a folly and that, in the end, they're not important. Yes, we need to cure cancer, but the arts are also important and they deserve respect.

We're in the midst of a national conversation about race and racial equity. Is your organization doing anything internally or externally to address racial inequity?

Recent events remind us that every generation bears the responsibility to preserve the progress made in the past and continue the struggle for equality and social justice for all. City Opera was founded as the "People's Opera," and its greatest successes have always come from reflecting the people and values of the city around it—a thriving city of immigrants, and the most diverse community in the world.

City Opera's history of diversity and inclusion goes back to its very earliest days, and is among its proudest traditions. The company was only in its second year when Todd

Duncan took the stage as the first African-American in history to perform a lead role in a major opera company. Not long after that, City Opera General Director Laszlo Halasz got death threats for hiring Camilla Williams to sing *Madama Butterfly*. Halasz's response was that he had hired "a voice, not a color." Seven decades later, that is still the City Opera casting policy, and it results in the ethnically diverse casts that are a hallmark of the company. It's no longer revolutionary to see diversity on the operatic stage, but when a talented young singer of color has a breakout success at City Opera, as Brandie Sutton did this season in *La Campana Sommersa*, it makes me proud that we are continuing this important legacy.

English-language works have always been a focus of the company in its mission to bring opera to a wider audience. Now, in 2017, a quarter of New York City households are Spanish-speaking, and we are reflecting that with our Spanish-language series, *Ópera en Español*. This season's Spanish-language offering is *Cruzar la Cara de la Luna*, a Mariachi opera about the struggles of family divided by the Mexico-U.S. border. It could not be more timely, or more relevant.

With a new administration and Congress, what role should the nonprofit sector and organizations like yours play over the next two to four years?

I don't have a lot of faith that this administration is going to rally behind our industry. I think we need to approach them in a nontraditional way and create a situation that they find more appealing. For instance, if they're compelled to reduce funding for the National Endowment for the Arts, then give patrons a larger tax break to help the people who want to support the arts to do so. That way, when I go to a prospective donor I can say, "You can help us here, and you'll get a dollar-for-dollar write-off." Resisting and protesting has its place, but with all the smart people who support this industry, we should be able to come up with a different business angle. We need a creative business plan that allows individuals to support the arts without creating the kind of government expenditures that fiscal conservatives find so objectionable. There can still be some sort of approval stamp from the government, but it'll be much more privatized. Give the private sector greater ability to donate on a larger scale through a better tax break.

After the 2016 election, *The New York Times* reported, "the widening political divergence between cities and small-town America also reflects a growing alienation between the two groups, and a sense—perhaps accurate—that their fates are not connected." What role should the nonprofit sector play in helping the two groups find common ground?

There is a perception that New York is disconnected from the rest of America, which is a shame. New York has so much to offer, not just to New Yorkers but to the whole country, but it can be overwhelming if you're not from here. I think that for many, there's a fear of urban centers, but it's combined with a fascination; that's why people go to Disneyland to pretend they're in Paris, or go to Vegas to stay at the Venetian. It's cheaper to go to the actual Venice, but they're afraid.

I think you can get people from rural America to feel connected to the larger towns in their region, and then eventually with larger cities, and the performing arts can play a role in that. A city like Toledo has a smaller opera company and symphony that locals can connect with, and then you have a little cross-promotion with a slightly larger city like Columbus. Then from Columbus you connect with Cincinnati, and then Chicago. I think you have to bring them along in baby steps.

If there were one thing you could say to your colleagues who are leading grant-making foundations, what would it be?

You should focus on the merits of the applicant and streamline the process. Pay attention to organizations that have great merit, and find a way to expedite their processes so that if you have a great idea, you can get it funded quickly. Be willing to take risks. In the 1960s, the Ford Foundation funded a season of all-American operas at City Opera, which was unheard of. But that's why today we have *The Crucible*, *Susannah*, *Baby Doe* and other operas that are now in the mainstream. Those operas needed to be put in front of the public, but it couldn't be done without help, because new and unfamiliar works are always a difficult sell. But with the Ford Foundation's help, City Opera was able to reduce ticket prices and cultivate an audience for these important works.

The best jokes have some truth behind them. What is your favorite joke about your profession or the nonprofit sector or anything that's relevant to what we've talked about?

"Life is short, opera is long." I think I saw that on a T-shirt in San Francisco.

On days when I question my own sanity, I remember a quip from the conductor Franz Schalk, who said, "Every theater is an insane asylum, but an opera theater is the ward for the incurables." But the most insightful joke I know about the opera is probably the oldest. It's from Molière, who said, "Of all the noises known to man, opera is the most expensive."

CHAPTER 11

Muhammed Chaudhry

*President and CEO, Silicon Valley
Education Foundation*

Muhammed Chaudhry serves as president and CEO for the Silicon Valley Education Foundation (SVEF). Under his stewardship, SVEF has become the leading education non-profit preparing students for college and careers in Silicon Valley. The foundation is dedicated to elevating scholastic achievement in science, technology, engineering and math-ematics (STEM). Under his leadership, it has forged strong partnerships with the industry and education community to develop innovative programs to support public education.

Chaudhry is a board member of the Californians Dedicated to Education Foundation and serves on the National Science Foundation's Advisory Committee. He is also on the Advisory Board of Silicon Valley Reads and California Consortium of Education Foundation. His personal interests include golf, long-distance running and volunteering with various philanthropic causes.

He previously held management positions in brand marketing with the Clorox Company and Dazzle Multimedia. He holds a B.S. degree in business administration from San Jose State University and is a graduate of the Stanford Executive Leadership Program. He resides in San Jose with his wife and two children.

Silicon Valley Education Foundation

The Silicon Valley Education Foundation is a nonprofit resource and advocate for students and educators. It drives scholastic achievement in the critical areas of STEM, by combining resources and partnerships to provide innovative academic programs.

A catalyst for policy solutions in public education, it is an advocate for public education in Silicon Valley. The region has California's sixth-largest school system, with more than 370,000 students and 18,000 teachers. The foundation's goal is to promote and support STEM education, and to make Silicon Valley the leading region in California for students graduating from high school academically prepared for post-secondary success. This is defined by the number of students completing the A-G course requirements (the University of California/California State University minimum entrance requirements).

The foundation's multifaceted strategy includes: 1) operating programs focused on STEM that impact students directly, and strategically targeting gateway courses such as middle and high school math, to make sure students stay on course for high school graduation and college success; 2) working directly with school districts to reform policies that are holding students back from achieving their full potential; and 3) working with the business and high-tech communities to bring innovative education technology into the classroom, ensuring that students are gaining the skills they need to succeed in the 21st century economy.

Muhammed Chaudhry

Who has had the greatest influence on you as a professional?

There isn't one person, but a group of leaders that I turn to. Some are John W. Thompson at Microsoft, a lawyer named Larry Sonsini, Wilson Santini and Paul Humphries, the president at Flex. They have taught me sound business principles and approaches.

Thus far, what have been the worst and best events in your life, and what did those experiences teach you?

The best was when we had our twins. As I watched the progression of their learning, I learned so much that has transferred to the workplace. I saw how learning happens and what a good teacher can do. I learned how to develop a growth mindset and how to invest time every day. I am much more focused and disciplined now, and it has made our organization better.

The worst thing that happened to me was when I was let go from a job in college. I was devastated, but I learned perspective and perseverance. I did not repeat the same mistakes and came to the conclusion of what I wanted to do and how. I learned that more can be accomplished with a greater sense of humility than through bravado leadership.

What, if anything, keeps you up at night?

My mom passed a year ago, and it really put life in perspective. I wrote an open letter in the local paper, and I still think about her at night.

In business, the thing that keeps me up at night is the speed of execution. How do we help more kids faster? How do we make it work?

What advice would you give to your peers in the nonprofit sector about building an organization or scaling with the programs and operations?

Don't try to do it all. You need absolute focus and must stay true to the core mission in order to build up. We wanted to do more. We wanted to create programs for all STEM subjects (science, technology, engineering and mathematics), and our chairman of the board told us to pick one. We picked math, and just focusing on that put the entire organization behind this. The program was elevated and now, seven years later, we're serving up to 5,000 kids. We're now developing a program to work with teachers. We're driving change at a level that is important and impactful, changing the student trajectory and making better math teachers. Our goal is to serve 100,000 kids. We chose not to chase money. We had a donor interested in another subject, but we had to walk away and stay focused on math. Everyone is thinking about the same thing from different angles.

What is your philosophy of life?

I'm very driven and competitive, but I come from a religious background of fairness and justice. I stay true to that background in the way I conduct myself.

What is the greatest misconception about you?

People misconceive what my motivation is. I am highly driven toward doing the most good in the shortest amount of time possible. How to solve intractable problems is what drives me every day.

What is the most important thing you tell young people who are thinking about making careers in the nonprofit sector?

To understand why it is they do what they do, and to gain the skills to do it. It may not be offered by the nonprofit sector. They might have to work in fund-raising or human resources to gain some experience.

What new opportunities do you see for your organization in the next five years?

There are a lot of opportunities for scaling. Now that we have evidence for the math program, I see us reaching 100,000 kids instead of 5,000. New politics will affect us and we have a lot of challenges ahead, but we must understand the changes and continue to push. We need a laser-focused execution.

We are in the midst of a national conversation about race and racial equity. What is your organization doing, both internally and externally, to address racial inequity?

We spend a lot of time on the achievement gap between whites and minorities. There's a 30-point gap. We are working with corporations who are not comfortable talking about policy changes and need direct intervention. There is a great threat to religious freedom as well now. Race and religion have become related.

The best jokes have some truth behind them. What is your favorite joke about your profession or the nonprofit sector?

How does Moses make coffee? He brews it.

What is the one thing you would say to your colleagues who are leading nonprofits seeking foundation funding?

Before you seek funding, truly seek agreement on what dial you want to move. Agree on the measurement and then the solution. Tell me what dial you want to move and what number, if moved, would have the best impact. For me, it's the number of students that graduate from high school having completed the courses required for college.

If there were one thing you could say to your colleagues who are leading grant-making foundations, what would it be?

You have such an immense responsibility to make sure you know your dial, your true north and what else you can contribute besides money. Wisdom, wealth and work go beyond money. Be passionate about your mission and how you achieve it.

CHAPTER 12

Bill Shore

Founder and CEO, Share Our Strength

Bill Shore is the founder and CEO of Share Our Strength, a national nonprofit that is ending childhood hunger in the United States through the No Kid Hungry campaign. He founded Share Our Strength in 1984 with his sister, Debbie Shore, and a $2,000 cash advance on a credit card. Since then, it has raised and invested more than $600 million in the fight against hunger, and has won the support of national leaders in business, government, health and education, sports and entertainment.

From 2014 to 2015, Shore served as a congressional appointee to the National Commission on Hunger, a group tasked with finding innovative ways to end hunger in the United States. From 1978 to 1987, he served on the senatorial and presidential campaign staffs of former U.S. Senator Gary Hart (D-Colorado). From 1988 to 1991, he served as chief of staff for former U.S. Senator Robert Kerrey (D-Nebraska).

Shore is the author of four books focused on social change, including *Revolution of the Heart* (Riverhead Press, 1995), *The Cathedral Within* (Random House, 1999), *The Light of Conscience* (Random House, 2004) and most recently, *The Imaginations of Unreasonable Men* (PublicAffairs, 2010).

He was named one of America's Best Leaders in 2005 by *U.S. News and World Report*. In 2011, the Jefferson Awards Foundation presented him with the S. Roger Horchow Award for Greatest Public Service.

Share Our Strength

Share Our Strength was founded with the belief that everyone has a strength to share in the global fight against hunger and poverty, and that in these shared strengths lie solutions. Thirty years later, the organization has raised more than $604 million to combat hunger and poverty and is renowned for finding scalable, pragmatic solutions to social problems.

Today, it is focused on ending hunger in the United States through the No Kid Hungry campaign (NoKidHungry.org).

Since the launch of the campaign in 2010, the organization has connected 3 million more kids with school breakfast, added 40,000 new summer meals sites to feed kids when school is out, and continued to be a strategic grant-maker helping kids and their families in all 50 states. Today, one-third fewer children are facing hunger than before the campaign began.

In 1983, the organization launched Cooking Matters (CookingMatters.org), a program that empowers low-income families with the skills to stretch their food budgets so that their children can get healthy meals at home. Since its launch, Cooking Matters has reached more than 500,000 families through its courses, grocery store tours and mobile, online and educational tools.

In 1984, Share Our Strength launched Community Wealth Partners, a consulting firm that helps change agents tackle their community's most daunting challenges. Twenty years later, Community Wealth Partners has helped diverse, inspiring change agents make lasting progress in their organizations and communities.

Bill Shore

At what point in your life did you realize you wanted to make a career in the nonprofit sector, and what was it that made you decide this?

I always had a public service orientation. Our father was a district administrative assistant for a congressman. His life and our immediate environment were all about serving constituents. It was a political family, so I knew I wanted to work in Congress. That led to wanting to start Share Our Strength with my sister. It was probably a number of factors coming together, including Senator Gary Hart losing in the 1984 Democratic presidential primaries [after I worked on his campaign], and the Ethiopian famine. It was not a conscious decision about a particular vehicle.

Thus far, what have been the worst and best events in your life, and what did those experiences teach you?

The best things were certainly my children and learning to be present as a human being to other people's needs. The worst thing was seeing my family struggle when my first marriage ended in divorce. Work and family balance is important. I find that my work benefits from spending more time with my family, from being more deeply rooted in other people's needs. When I leave early to go to my son's soccer game, I know it will benefit my work.

What, if anything, is keeping you up at night?

I wonder if we are aiming too low. I worry about failure of imagination. If you're working your tail off, but you've aimed too low, that seems like a terrible waste. I think about potential blind spots or what we are missing that we should be tackling. For many years at Share Our Strength, we made grants to other organizations. We hadn't imagined that we could end childhood hunger.

I always pick problems that are big enough to matter and small enough to win. We have made enormous progress. There is a line of sight to the end, and we're starting to ask if there's something else we should be doing. No Kid Hungry was developed about eight years ago. The visibility of that brand has become much more visible than Share Our Strength. In the next six to eight years, I believe we will have achieved No Kid Hungry in the United States.

What is your definition of happiness?

My wife always says that moments of grace are having the people around you that matter the most, like your family or closest friends, and being present to it in the moment. To quote Kurt Vonnegut, "I urge you to please notice when you are happy, and exclaim or murmur or think at some point, 'If this isn't nice, I don't know what is.' It's a terrible waste to be happy and not notice it."

What is the most important thing you tell young people who are thinking about making careers in the nonprofit sector?

I strongly believe that you should aim toward what you want to do and not feel you have to take a lot of detours to have your ticket punched. I talk to people who think they should make some money first, and they get trapped doing that. They never get around to being in the nonprofit sector. It doesn't make sense to defer your passion.

What new opportunities do you see for your organization in the next five years?

There is an abundance of opportunities, and the hard part is for us to pick. There are other populations who suffer from hunger, like veterans or families. There are things we have done that would be applicable in other parts of the world. Getting to the root causes of poverty is much more difficult than solving hunger. We'll be thinking about this over the next few years.

We are in the midst of a national conversation about race and racial equity. What is your organization doing, both internally and externally, to address racial inequity?

Since the election, bigotry, racism and misogyny have resurfaced in the national conversation. We have to make our values explicit. When we talk about No Kid Hungry, we have to say: no Muslim kid, no gay kid, no straight kid. A lot of us didn't think we would be having this conversation. The populations we serve don't have an equal path to access opportunity. Our work goes right to the heart of that question. We just had a meeting about how we are not where we want to be. About 20 percent of our senior staff are people of color. We asked and answered questions to determine how many privileges we had and to gauge people's reactions. It is something we are working on.

If there were one thing you could say to your colleagues who are leading grant-making foundations, what would it be?

Take the long view on leadership. I am much less interested in proposals than in the leadership of the organization. Take a gamble on somebody if they could blossom as a leader. Make bets and take risks on people. When I think about what it took to start Share Our Strength, we needed some folks to take a gamble on us.

CHAPTER 13

Campaign on Many Fronts

It stands to reason that complex social problems would require complex answers involving many different actors and institutions. In fact, many of our interviewees realized along the way that they had to involve other sectors, such as government, in achieving their goals.

Here are the steps we identified as hallmarks of most successful social change campaigns.

A. Find Common Ground

At this writing, it is sometimes difficult to believe that the people of the United States will find enough common ground to save the nation as a democracy.

Our interviewees believe it is imperative to find common ground to bring about social change. Dan Gross of the Brady Campaign to Prevent Gun Violence puts it this way.

"We are not here to make social commentary on guns, and we don't come out of hatred of guns or people who own them. We come here with a single-minded desire to prevent people from getting shot. That has led us to the insights based on common ground that almost every American shares, and which have the potential to make this country and everyone who lives here much safer."

Gross' background is in advertising. In 1997, when he was 30 years old and J. Walter Thompson's youngest partner, his brother was shot and almost killed on the observation deck of the Empire State Building, when a gunman opened fire on a crowd, killing six people.

Gross studied the issue and applied his training to thinking about the issue before he jumped into the fray. He knew he wanted to do something to stanch gun violence, but he realized he needed to devise a way of reframing the conventional approach to the subject. He used "insight, marketing and communications" to develop a new way to talk about the issue. Can most Americans agree that they do not want their children to die from accidental gun violence in their home or the home of a friend? Of course they can. In other words, rather than simply a criminal justice issue, gun violence is a health and public safety issue.

Achieving this insight did not happen immediately. It took years. And it was only the beginning of the quest to prevent gun violence in the United States.

B. Change Social Norms

Social change is about creating a significant alteration over time in behavior patterns and cultural values and norms. By "significant" alteration, sociologists mean changes yielding *profound* social consequences in how people are expected to behave. Examples of significant social changes with long-term effects include the Industrial Revolution, the abolition of slavery and the feminist movement.

Changing social norms is a recurring theme among many of the change agents we interviewed. More nonprofits are using polling and social science to change social norms and to effect social change. This is about listening to what people are concerned about, and how messages are received, and tracking how effectively your organization's messages are reaching people.

Before coming to the Brady Campaign to Prevent Gun Violence in 2011, Dan Gross co-founded an organization called PAX, a center to prevent youth violence. He says, "In politics, the way you make change is by changing social norms and creating an appreciation for the real risks: to create indignation toward unsafe behavior and promote socially responsible behavior."

Building on this idea, PAX created a campaign known as the ASK (Asking Saves Kids) campaign. The campaign encourages parents, before they send their kids to play at a friend's home, to ask whether there is an unlocked gun in the house. Over time, more than 15 million parents have asked this question, creating a groundswell of awareness about the social irresponsibility of keeping an unlocked gun in your home.

C. Litigation Is One Tool

Many major social movements have a litigation component, from the civil rights movement to equal pay for women. Evan Wolfson, Founder of Freedom to Marry, is a leading advocate of using litigation to forward a cause. Wolfson worked on the issue of legalizing gay marriage in the United States for 32 years. A lawyer, he wrote his law school thesis in the 1980s on why gay people should have the freedom to marry. Eventually, he went to work for Lambda Legal, which is "committed to achieving full recognition of the civil rights of lesbians, gay men, bisexuals and transgender people and everyone living with HIV through impact litigation, education and public policy work."[8]

For years, from Lambda Legal, Wolfson litigated gay marriage cases. The organization had its first big win in Hawaii in 1998. Wolfson says, "It was the turning point that launched this ongoing global movement. … Lambda did its own fund-raising, and we were trying to get people to support the movement, and trying to build the kind of affirmative, sustained campaign that I'd always argued was necessary: which was that we needed to combine public education and political organizing with litigation in order to win."

Wolfson eventually left Lambda Legal to found Freedom to Marry, where, over a decade, he was able to develop public

---

8   Lambda Legal, home page. https://www.lambdalegal.org/ (accessed August 3, 2017).

education and political organizing that carried on the movement. This ultimately led to the Supreme Court decision in 2015 that declared gay marriage a Constitutional right.

D. Advocate, Advocate, Advocate

Stephen Heintz is president of the Rockefeller Brothers Fund, which "advances social change that contributes to a more just, sustainable and peaceful world."[9] Heintz notes, that although the fund is nonpartisan, it is political in the sense that it recognizes the importance of influencing the exercise of public power. "If you can influence public policy or private-sector behavior," he says, "you are really producing change, because those are the dominant sectors in our society."

Organizations need to understand that they are exercising their rights as U.S. citizens by engaging in advocacy. A nonprofit can spend up to 20 percent of its resources on such activities without jeopardizing its nonprofit status. Many, many nonprofits do not understand this. As a result, they do not engage in advocacy to advance their missions and generate greater social impact.

In our consulting practice, we train many staff and board members of nonprofits about advocacy, and they are always thrilled to know that they have the right to advocate for the causes they care about as long as they do not endorse any particular political candidate.

9   Rockefeller Brothers Fund, "Mission and Program Statement." http://www.rbf.org/programs/program-statement (accessed August 4, 2017).

In 2005, Andrew Rich, PhD, of Yale University, wrote an article in which he pointed out that conservative foundations had been far more effective in promoting conservative public policy than progressive foundations. He argued that this was not because conservative foundations provide more funding, but because they provided a different type of support. They supported advocacy and the marketing of ideas, and general operations, while progressive foundations provided more support for research and projects. He argued that conservative foundations were winning the war of ideas, and implementing those ideas through public policy think tanks.[10]

"By providing general operating support to policy institutes far more rarely than their conservative counterparts, progressive foundations make it difficult for progressive organizations to sustain operating staff and functions. As James Pierson, executive director of the conservative John M. Olin Foundation, commented of his liberal counterparts: 'The liberal foundations became too project-oriented—they support projects but not institutions. They flip from project to project. … We, on the other hand, support institutions. We provide the infrastructure for institutions.'"[11]

Since 2005, when Rich's article was published, progressive foundations have begun to enter the advocacy space in a much more vigorous way. The support of advocacy by these progressive foundations could help change policy and laws that hold back progress toward racial equity, poverty alleviation, criminal justice reform and many other causes.

---

10   Andrew Rich: "War of Ideas." *Stanford Social Innovation Review*, Spring 2005.
11   Ibid.

CHAPTER 14

Dan Gross

President, Brady Campaign to Prevent Gun Violence

Dan Gross is building on the Brady Campaign and Center's unrivaled legacy of success, with a goal of cutting gun deaths in the United States in half by 2025.

After his younger brother Matthew was critically injured in a mass shooting on the observation deck of the Empire State Building in February 1997, Gross, then the young-est-ever partner at the J. Walter Thompson ad agency, left a successful career in advertising to devote his life to the prevention of gun violence. He co-founded the Center to Prevent Youth Violence (originally PAX) in 1998, which, under his leadership, created and implemented life-saving public health and safety programs, including the ASK (Asking Saves Kids) and SPEAK UP campaigns.

Under his leadership, the Brady Campaign has announced the bold goal of cutting the number of U.S. gun deaths in half by 2025, based on an innovative and exciting strategy. Its central focus is on keeping guns from the people we all agree should not have them, through three impact-driven campaigns: first, a policy focus, "Finish the Job," ensuring that the life-saving background checks called for under the Brady Act are applied to all gun sales; second, to "Stop Bad Apple Gun Dealers," the 5 percent of gun dealers who supply 90 percent of all the guns used to commit crimes that are flowing into the most heavily impacted cities and communities; and lastly, to lead a new national conversation and change social norms around the real dangers of guns in the home, in order to prevent the homicides, suicides and unintentional shootings that happen every day.

Gross' work has been widely acclaimed and honored by organizations and individuals across the political spectrum. He served on Vice President Joe Biden's gun violence prevention task force, and worked closely with President Barack Obama and others in his administration on numerous important initiatives.

He earned a B.S. in psychology, with a minor in economics, with honors, from Tulane University. He lives in New York City with his wife and two children.

Brady Campaign to Prevent Gun Violence

The Brady Campaign seeks a safer future for every American—where dozens of gun deaths every day are no longer normal, and we can all live our lives free from the fear of being shot. Its aim is to reduce gun deaths by half by 2025, by rallying Americans around three focused, impact-driven solutions built entirely on the surprising common ground that already exists: that everyone wants to be safe, and that people who are a danger to themselves or others should not have access to guns.

Dan Gross

Who has had the greatest influence on you as a professional?

I've taken lessons from a lot of people throughout my career, but I would say Sarah and Jim Brady, the namesakes of this organization. Jim Brady was shot in the head and critically injured in the assassination attempt on President Ronald Reagan in 1981. In 1997, my brother was also shot in the head in an attack at the top of the Empire State Building I had just celebrated my 30th birthday the day before. Our dear friend Chris Burmeister was killed in the attack. My brother ended up in a coma and needed multiple brain surgeries. I remember being in Bellevue Hospital, thinking that I wanted to do something about this, but not wanting to rush into changing everything just because my family had experienced this tragedy.

I looked at this issue and knew that there were a lot of other folks with high-profile tragedies on the front page of *The New York Times*, on *60 Minutes*. People who all of a sudden got all their phone calls returned from national leaders. That happened to me as well. I was invited to meet President Bill Clinton in the Oval Office; it was very surreal in a lot of ways. But from the beginning, I remember being concerned that the interest in my family's story would fade with the headlines of the tragedy, and I wanted to do something that lasted and had a real impact. My orientation toward communication, insight and marketing led me to want to do my homework before I set out.

There were a lot of cautionary tales. I remember being in the hospital, and looking at my brother in a coma, being inspired by what Jim and Sarah Brady did. They're the only ones in the history of this issue who have, on a national level, made a massive change. I took my time and went to Washington D.C., and used my unique opportunity to meet with so many amazing leaders to figure out how to do something that was really going to make a difference.

A lot of people have had a very positive influence on me. When I met with Jim and Sarah Brady, it was their indomitable spirit and resolve that was profoundly inspiring. Then I started my own organization with a man named Talmage Cooley. We called it PAX, which turned into the Center to Prevent Youth Violence (CPYV). It quickly became very successful. The folks at J. Walter Thompson were very kind, and when I told them that I'd probably never return to my full-time position, they let me keep an office there and write a business plan for my new organization. They were very generous in many ways.

The organization was successful because we approached it the right way, and it tied into my genuine passion for marketing, communications and insight. It filled a vital role in addressing the gun violence purely as the public health and safety issue that it is, while steering completely clear of politics. We looked at it from the perspective of changing social norms. We created these public health and safety campaigns, and became best known for the ASK Campaign, which encourages parents to ask if there are guns in the homes where their kids play. Twenty million parents have started asking that lifesaving question as a result, and it remains an important part of Brady's efforts today.

In politics, the way you make change is by changing social norms and creating an appreciation for the real risks: to create indignation toward unsafe behavior and promote socially responsible behavior. The laws follow. That was the goal of CPYV.

During the period I was at CPYV, I watched as the Brady organization, which I now run, was declining. Seeing that broke my heart, but I had a lot of strong feelings about why it was happening. I didn't think it was communicating or framing the issue properly. All the clear pitfalls were there, like letting the politicians lead, chasing headlines after major tragedies, and then being surprised when the resolve for that change faded with those headlines. A number of times, this job became available, but we had so much momentum with my other organization. We became bigger than Brady in terms of fund-raising. We were doing work that was clearly changing things. Then in 2011, the job became available and an executive recruiter called. I realized I was drawing what I felt was an increasingly artificial line between framing things that are political and things that aren't. At the end of the day, whether the solution is a law or an education campaign, it's about keeping guns out of the hands of people whom we all agree shouldn't have them.

It's about framing things in terms of the ends rather than the means to the end, and figuring out and defining our common ground—what we all want. I told the headhunter I'd consider meeting with the Brady Board. I was in New York, and they were in D.C. and I didn't hold out a lot of hope we could make it work, for practical reasons; but I met with them, and it led to us working it out and my accepting this position. That led me to working closely with Jim and Sarah Brady and for the organization that bears their name, which was really the inspiration for my decision.

Obviously, the most fundamental impact anybody has had on my career is my brother, who is an inspiration to me every day. He's an amazing person and there's not a day that goes by that I don't think about him and what happened to him. I would never have thought of going into this field if it wasn't for what happened to him, but once I made that decision, it was Jim and Sarah Brady who had the biggest impact on me. When I met Sarah in the context of being the new president of the organization, she was at a place where she was incredibly frustrated with where this organization was. She felt it was rudderless and had lost its way. Supporters were dwindling. The organization was actually in much more financial trouble than I realized when I took the job, and all that affected Sarah. Although we knew each other before I took the job, she was kind of skeptical of me when I became president of Brady, which was something to grapple with, because she was the reason I was doing this in the first place!

One of the most rewarding parts of this job other than the progress we've made was the opportunity to work alongside Sarah and build a relationship that I'll treasure forever. It was one of the most meaningful relationships I've ever had in my life. Sarah was famously ornery, and because she started out skeptical of me, it made what we built so much more real and emotional. She gave me every reason to say, "Screw you." (I say that, because that's the kind of salty language she would have used.) She basically did say that to me initially. It could have worked like that: where she was just on the periphery and we'd have her namesake, and nobody would know any better. But instead, we built a real relationship that was so much more meaningful.

When Jim and Sarah moved to an assisted-living home in Virginia, I'd go there every week or two for dinner, and I'd meet Sarah's friends. She would brag about me, and even my wife and kids, like we were her own family. When she passed, it was devastating. Really, it is a devastating loss for our whole country, because Jim and Sarah were true American heroes. I don't think there are many Americans who have saved as many lives as Jim and Sarah Brady have—because of the Brady Bill, and what this organization has done. So much of what inspires me every day, as we go through good times and bad times, is knowing how much Sarah believed in the future of this organization and my leadership of it, and knowing that Sarah's support for me came from such a real place. It certainly wasn't out of any preconceived sense of obligation. It was because I proved it to her.

Thus far, what have been the worst and best events in your life, and what did those experiences teach you?

The worst thing is without a doubt my brother being shot. What happened to my brother has also created an opportunity that, if I want to be honest, I also have to say has also led to the best things that have happened in my career. It's sometimes difficult for me to reconcile this: Something so horrible has created an opportunity for me to do everything

I'm doing to make the world a better place. I wouldn't say what happened to my brother is the best thing that happened to me, but in that light, it created a lot of positive things.

One of the things that stuck out when I met Sarah Brady was her dogged determination and strength. She faced every day with such optimism. Prior to my brother being shot, I don't think I was capable of that. I didn't see myself single-mindedly focusing on one thing for my career. But now I know I can do it. Now I hear people accusing me of the same things that they used to accuse Sarah of. People ask how I can be so optimistic. I'm almost offended by that, because optimism can be confused with being unrealistic, but I believe that my optimism is entirely realistic. I consider myself a strategic, pragmatic optimist. I pride myself on a balance between idealism and pragmatism, and I'm driven by both.

When I was in advertising, I honestly didn't know I was capable of working this hard. Last year, I was in 37 states. I worked through almost every weekend. I used to think I needed eight hours of sleep. Sometimes I wake up in the middle of the night, especially during intense times, and I know I'm never going back to bed, so I'll work or write or think. I'm always thinking about this issue and strategy. I never knew I was capable of wholeheartedly devoting myself and working as hard on something as I have on this.

But really the best thing to happen to me is a toss-up between meeting my wife and my kids being born. My wife and kids teach me things every day. My relationship with my wife works because it is so complementary. She looks at the world in a different way, one that I deeply admire. I approach everything with a fire and passion. She's passionate and emotional, but she doesn't need to be liked. People just like her because she is who she is. In the world of politics, almost everyone I meet is the opposite of that, so she teaches me to be more like her.

One of the great challenges associated with being so passionate and devoted to my job is that it becomes a tough balance between work and family. It's really difficult to ever be offline. I struggle with that balance every day, to make sure we spend enough time together as a family so I don't miss my kids growing up. My wife's amazing devotion to our kids and family while I have this job is so unbelievably admirable and inspiring—and all this while she has her own full-time job. She's also one of the funniest people I know. We laugh a lot, which is a real key when your life is as complicated as ours.

What, if anything, keeps you up at night?

What keeps me up most at night is opportunity, not dread or challenges. There's so much work to do. If anything has the potential to keep me up at night, it's that there are only so many hours in a day, and there's so much to do. That crosses over into challenges when we're not all paddling in the same direction on this issue and in this movement. I genuinely believe all the prominent organizations that are working on this issue have so much value to add. We will never be monolithic like the gun lobby, because we are not driven by an industry. We have to behave like a healthy ecosystem, where if you fulfill a vital role, you'll survive and flourish.

Worrying about anything other than focusing on our common goal undermines our ability to do that work.

I think the presidential election is obviously keeping a lot of people up at night. That was certainly devastating on many levels. But I'm up at night, because I want everybody to appreciate that we still have the same momentum that we had on November 7. I was in New York at the Javits Center on the night of the election. That's something that I never want to go through again. I got on a plane the next day with a pit in my stomach, and went to California and Arizona to rally the troops. I was saying that the election "sucked," but that we still have momentum and an opportunity that we created together. People appreciated that message. We just need to keep hammering it home, with the public and with the media—and continue to define ourselves by what we are for, not what we are against.

What is your definition of happiness, or, what is your philosophy of life?

When my family and dearest friends are happy, I'm happy. Some of my happiest memories will always be just being in the car with my family, singing along with the radio, seeing everybody getting along.

I had the opportunity to take my son to the White House for the last holiday party, and he got to meet President Barack Obama and the first lady, which gave me so much joy. Later on, we were milling about the White House, and a senior adviser I work closely with came running out of nowhere. She got down on her knees in front of my son and said, "I know you don't get to see your dad as much as you should, but

I just want you to know your dad is a real hero." To watch my son's reaction to that, honestly, meant more to me than meeting the president, because I don't get to be with my family as much as I'd like. So it makes me really happy to see when they're proud of me and think I'm making a difference. The happiness comes when we spend time together, and I get fulfillment in knowing they take pride in what I do.

What is the most important thing you tell young people who are thinking about making careers in the nonprofit sector?

I tell them how thoughtful I was about what I did. A lot of people assume that my brother was shot and I said I was going to do something. Then I was thrown into the spotlight, and the rest is history. It becomes a dangerous story when it's romanticized like that, so I want people to appreciate how thoughtful I was about it. I want them to understand that I made my decision because of an opportunity to apply both skills that I had through my previous career and, most importantly, things I was genuinely passionate about professionally. When people hear that, they assume I'm talking about passion for the gun issue, because my brother was shot, but I'm actually talking about communications, marketing and consumer insight.

I think empathy is the most important skill to have in advertising and communication, maybe life in general. It's trying to put yourself in the other person's shoes, and see the world from their perspective. Selling anything, whether it's a product or a cause, doesn't work unless you tap into something real about the person you are trying to reach. I always advise young people about the importance of empathy and listening, and I advise them to do something they're genuinely passionate about. The rest will figure itself out. Don't go into the nonprofit sector only because you want to make the world a better place or you feel you genuinely care about some issue. Do it if it is an opportunity to leverage skills you have and things you like to do. That's ultimately the way you will make a difference. Always listen carefully to people. Read between the lines and be honest with yourself.

When we wind up making bad hires, it's almost always because people aren't being honest with themselves about what they want to do. I can think of numerous instances where people have looked me in the eye, and I could see they were convincing themselves that this was something they really wanted to do because they were passionate about the issue, not about our approach to it. So be honest with yourself about why you want to do it. Having a passion for an issue is the place to start, but it can't end there. Base it on things you enjoy and things you're good at.

What new opportunities do you see for Brady in the next five years?

Our fundamental challenge over the coming years is to go big or go home. We have a goal to double the size of the organization in three years, and to cut gun deaths in half by 2025. We have three campaigns through which we are working to do that, with clear goals and benchmarks. Another challenge is to grow this movement into a true cultural force, as we have seen on other issues, which transcends affiliations with individual organizations. For too long, our movement has gotten caught up in these petty differences that the whole world doesn't see. At the end of the day, what we need to do is get millions more people engaged and ratchet up the intensity.

The reason we finally pushed this issue to the brink of a tipping point is because we're not just talking about ourselves. It isn't just the usual suspects like me, victims or leaders of organizations like Brady anymore. Kim Kardashian is tweeting about it. I realize it's kind of a random example, but it's the kind of pop-culture saturation we need to really move the needle. No one organization is going to change things by itself. It shouldn't matter what T-shirt someone is wearing when they meet with their legislator or who they say they are from when they call their office or show up at a town hall meeting. It just matters that they do those things. That's what we've always needed to engage the public on a real cultural level.

If there were one thing you could say to your colleagues leading grant-making organizations, what would it be?

A lot of people look at this issue with a sense of hopelessness and despair, and I want them to appreciate that we have a genuine opportunity to achieve our audacious goal of cutting gun deaths in half. Brady has the right strategy and programs to do it. I would tell them to give me the opportunity to prove it and to evaluate everything that we do through the lens of the impact we can make. We're not here to make social commentary on guns, and we don't come out of hatred of guns or people who own them. We come here with a single-minded desire to prevent people from getting shot. That has led us to the insights based on common ground that almost every American shares, and which have the potential to make this country and everyone who lives here much safer.

CHAPTER 15

Stephen Heintz

President, Rockefeller Brothers Fund

Stephen Heintz has been president of the Rockefeller Brothers Fund since 2001. Before joining the RBF, he held top leadership positions in both the nonprofit and public sectors. He was founding president of Dēmos, a public policy research and advocacy organization working to enhance the vitality of American democracy and promote more broadly shared prosperity. Prior to founding Dēmos, he served as executive vice president and chief operating officer of the EastWest

Institute, where he worked on issues of economic reform, civil society development and international security. Based in Prague from 1990 through 1997, he worked extensively throughout Central and Eastern Europe and the newly independent states. He devoted the first 15 years of his career to politics and government service in the state of Connecticut, where he served as commissioner of economic development and commissioner of social welfare. In 1988, he helped draft and secure passage by Congress of the Family Support Act, the first major effort to reform the U.S. welfare system.

He currently serves on the boards of the EastWest Institute, the Rockefeller Archive Center and *The American Prospect* magazine. He is a member of the Council on Foreign Relations and a fellow of the American Academy of Arts and Sciences. *The NonProfit Times* has consistently named him one of the 50 most influential leaders of the nonprofit sector. In 2012, President Bronisław Komorowski of Poland granted him the Officer's Cross, Order of Merit of the Republic of Poland for his contributions to building civil society and democratic institutions in Poland.

Rockefeller Brothers Fund

Founded in 1940, the Rockefeller Brothers Fund (RBF) advances social change that contributes to a more just, sustainable and peaceful world.

Its grant-making is organized around three themes: democratic practice, peacebuilding and sustainable development. Although it pursues its three program interests in a variety of geographic contexts, it has identified several specific locations on which to concentrate cross-programmatic attention. It refers to these as "pivotal places": subnational areas, nation states, or cross-border regions that have special importance for RBF's substantive concerns, and whose future will have disproportionate significance for the future of a surrounding region, an ecosystem or the world. The RBF currently works in two pivotal places: southern China and the western Balkans. The Charles E. Culpeper Arts and Culture program nurtures a vibrant and inclusive arts community in New York City. These programs reflect board and staff assessment of the challenges facing today's increasingly interdependent world on which strategic philanthropy and the RBF's accumulated grant-making experience can have a meaningful impact.

Through its grant-making, the RBF supports efforts to expand knowledge, clarify values and critical choices, nurture creative expression and shape public policy. Its programs are intended to develop leaders, strengthen institutions, engage citizens, build community and foster partnerships that include government, business and civil society. Respect for cultural diversity and ecological integrity pervades the RBF's activities. It also manages the Pocantico Center as part of an agreement with the National Trust for Historic Preservation, using it as a venue for conferences and meetings on critical issues related to the RBF's mission.

Stephen Heintz

Who has had the greatest influence on you as a professional?

There have been so many wonderful mentors in my life. The very first was an American businessman turned politician turned statesman named Chester Bowles. I was a senior at Yale, an American Studies major with a focus on American diplomatic history. I was required to write a senior thesis using original research. I was struggling to find a topic. David Halberstam, in *The Best and the Brightest*, introduced me to Chester Bowles.

Bowles was deputy secretary of state in the first year of the Kennedy administration. The reason he was of interest to Halberstam was that Bowles was the outlier on the team. He opposed the invasion of Cuba and was reluctant to see America getting more deeply involved in Vietnam. He kept expressing contrary views to the new frontiersmen of the Kennedy administration. Bobby Kennedy in particular found it irritating, and they ultimately pushed Bowles out of the State Department leadership at the end of 1961 and sent him back to India to be ambassador a second time. I found out that Bowles had left all his papers to Yale. I had an extraordinary experience writing this long manuscript about his experiences, and I got to know him. I went to interview him, Dean Rusk, Ted Sorensen and other key players in that story.

Bowles, as he had so often done throughout his career, took me under his wing, although he was long since retired and living on the shores of the Connecticut River. I started my own career immediately after that, in politics and state government in Connecticut, where Bowles had been governor. He became an important mentor at a very early age for me, and a very late age for him.

The second was a governor of Connecticut, Bill O'Neill, for whom I ended up working. He somehow had the crazy idea when I was 29 years old that he wanted me to be state social services commissioner. This frankly scared the death out of me, and I tried to talk him out of it. He laughed and said, "Well, I appreciate your modesty, but you're the guy I want." I said, "Well, all right, governor, if you're crazy enough to appoint me, I guess I'm crazy enough to accept." We had a really wonderful working relationship that I learned a great deal from.

Now fast-forward many years. David Rockefeller became an important mentor and leader to me over these past 15 years. It was an extraordinary privilege to get to know him in the last part of his life and to understand how much responsibility we have to extend his and his brothers' legacy.

Thus far, what have been the worst and best events in your life, and what did those experiences teach you?

The worst was a diagnosis of a rare blood cancer: myelodysplastic syndrome, a rare form of leukemia. The only thing that prevents it from being fatal is a bone-marrow transplant. I had what I now refer to as my involuntary sabbatical in 2012. I went into hospital in March and wasn't back to work until late October. During that period, I had lots of ups and downs and learned a lot.

It turns out it was a wonderful experience, as odd as that sounds, because you learn so much about yourself and about what is important. A community of people rushed to support me, starting with my wonderful spouse and my son, who was 10 years old. The support radiated out in endless concentric circles. It was humbling and life-giving. An anonymous donor someplace on this planet, without knowing me, gave stem cells that ended up saving my life.

I came out of it absolutely committed, saying to myself, "You know what, I can really make something out of this." I thought long and hard about what that might be. I thought, I'm 60 years old, and if I want to think about trying to take on one other big challenge in my life, it's the time to do it.

That was one way to look at it. The other way was to try to do big things with the opportunity I had. My wife and I talked about it a lot, and I talked about it with members of the board here, including members of the Rockefeller family. I concluded I would try to carry on here at the Rockefeller Brothers Fund in a way that would have as much impact as possible.

I had also decided that to the extent I could work and think and read and write, I was going to do that. That was the biggest benefit of time off. I could do a lot of reading when I was unable to do anything else. Because of my roots in American democracy, my global career and government experience, I decided I would spend the year thinking about the state of American democracy.

I came back to the RBF with a concept I called the National Purpose Initiative. I reached the conclusion that

Americans have lost the sense of shared national purpose. Sometimes, purpose is thrust on you, as in World War II, and sometimes purpose emerges, as in the civil rights movement. I began to think that what Americans needed was a renewed sense of shared national purpose that people could commit to in a civic way.

We decided ultimately not to implement a big initiative under that umbrella, but work on a variety of things we hope are contributing to something that might emerge along the way. The timing obviously now seems more urgent than ever. Throughout my illness, a tremendous amount of learning came out of what otherwise could have been a very bad experience.

On the good news side, there's just so much. I want to try to avoid clichés, but of course meeting my wife. Then, having a son later in life. We have this 15-year-old boy, who is such a joy. Coming to the RBF seemed to me like an impossible dream. But the foundation hired me because they appreciated the way I was thinking. I brought this experience in government and politics for 15 years and 10 years' experience in the nonprofit sector, most of it international. Then I founded a significant domestic nonprofit organization, Dēmos. Those kinds of skills end up being really useful running a foundation, in particular having the experience of being a grant-seeker.

When my staff members get tired, I occasionally remind them how uncomfortable it is to be on the other side of the table, and that it is our grantees that are doing the really hard work. They are on the front lines of social change;

we are here to enable and support them. We need to be nimble, responsive and helpful in ways that go beyond the grant dollars.

The combination of these experiences was a great training ground for me. I can exercise my intellectual interests in domestic and international affairs in a foundation that is ready to take risks, be bold and carry on a tradition that the family has been leading for five generations. The experience with leukemia reaffirmed that this is exactly the right place for me to be.

What, if anything, keeps you up at night these days?

The fate of the planet. One of the gifts this place has given me is to learn more about climate change. Well before I was even aware that climate change was a looming threat, the foundation was at work on global warming. It was one of the very first foundations to want to know more about what scientists were saying about climate change. This problem is urgent, and happening more rapidly than the scientists originally predicted. We are approaching certain tipping points that could happen almost anytime. The results could be devastating.

I have come to think that the three core operating systems of modern civilization are showing signs of obsolescence and proving anachronistic in the 21st century: the nation-state system, carbon-fueled capitalism and representative democracy.

The nation-state system is really a 17th-century invention. Nation states are still important, but they are incapable of solving global problems on their own. This is clearly a major political issue in our country right now. How do we manage the notion of reduced national sovereignty and the need for increased, shared sovereignty? We have an administration in Washington that rejects that notion and wants to go back to a nation state-based concept of sovereignty. The second system developed after the invention of the steam engine in the 1800s. The Industrial Revolution created enormous progress and wealth, but it was based on the extraction and burning of fossil fuels, starting with coal and moving into oil and natural gas. That has been a huge boon to mankind since 1800, but it is threatening the future of the planet. That operating system has to be radically reinvented.

The third system is representative democracy. Society has gotten so big, the body politic has gotten so diverse and media markets have changed so profoundly. Today, our political system seems neither very representative or genuinely democratic. The power and influence of money have grown so dramatically that the Enlightenment notions of representative democracy are also showing signs of inadequacy. All three of these core operating systems need to be reinvented for the 21st century. I'm basically an optimist, and I think we have to be optimists. The question is whether we will marshal the human capacity to reinvent these life-sustaining, civilization-sustaining systems.

What is your definition of happiness, or, what is your philosophy of life?

Happiness is being able to have a positive impact on those around you, starting with your family and friends.

Watching my son develop as a young man is a profound source of joy—seeing how the combination of genes and his life experiences are shaping a caring, thoughtful person. Working in a field that is about caring—caring for others, caring for society, caring for the planet—is an enormously joyful experience.

What is the greatest misconception about you?

Somebody once asked me if I wear starched underwear. That was a long time ago. I grew up in a lovely suburb of New York that was essentially an all-white suburb: There was one African-American family, and the mother of the family was an opera singer. I went to a public school because I was living in a wealthy community where the public schools were great. I went to Yale. I used to wear a suit and necktie all the time. So I think people may assume that I might be either a little more conservative philosophically or personally than I am and maybe less approachable than I hope I am.

What's the most important thing you tell young people who are thinking about making careers in the nonprofit sector?

I tell them two things. One is to get experience on the front lines. Go to places where nonprofit organizations are engaged with people on the ground, trying to help them solve problems and create better lives. The second is to work and live overseas. Get some perspective on this country by seeing the rest of the world—not just by traveling, but by living it.

What new opportunities do you see for this foundation for the next five years?

One of the things that's been exciting here in the last couple of years is that we've been having a very explicit conversation with our trustees and our staff about risk. This was the subject of a two-hour conversation at our March board meeting this year. Risk is a fact of life, and we all manage it in a variety of ways. Some risk you can anticipate, so you plan for the potential of those risks, you get fire insurance. Some risk you can't anticipate.

The question is: How do you respond to risk as it happens? Some are considered risks we all take. In investing money, we're taking risk. We study, we learn, we listen, we get advice and we might make an investment and hope that it's going to produce a certain return. We certainly hope we're not going to lose money, but sometimes we do. In grant-making, we're taking risks too. Because we're betting on people, we're betting on institutions. Let me step back and say, philanthropy is a very small sector. American foundations give away about $60 billion a year, a significant sum of money except when you compare it to the scale of the problems we are addressing.

Just look at all federal, state and local government spending in the United States. It is about $7 trillion, and the U.S. gross domestic product is about $17 trillion. So $50 billion to $60 billion is really a small amount of money. A lot of that is being used for what we might traditionally think of as more charitable things, not for social change. The amount that's going into social change work is small, and some of that is being used internationally.

We have the challenge of trying to figure out how to leverage the resources—the small resources that we've got—to have the biggest possible effect. The simple metaphor I use is acupuncture, something I had a little experience with during my recovery. We have these tiny needles, and the question is: Where do we insert the needles with the expectation that we might trigger some larger systemic change? And that leads you to think: It's not just about the money. It's about other assets that we can invest: reputation, convening power, knowledge, capacity-building and risk. Sometimes, if you want to create major change, you have to take extra risk to do it. We've been trying to think about our risk posture in a 360-degree way that looks at all those factors.

What are the risks we take with our endowment? For example, what risk did we take when we made the complicated and important decision to divest from all fossil fuels, especially given that fossil fuels were the original source of the Rockefeller wealth? That was a risky decision. A lot of investment advisers were saying, "You're excluding a very significant share of the global economy and saying you're not going to participate in it. That will limit the places you could go for the financial returns you're trying to achieve."

It was not only a risk in our investments, it was a risk for the Rockefeller family and the brand name. But it turned out to be something that paid enormous benefits. So I think that this is an opportunity. The opportunities are to be bolder, to take more carefully and prudently considered risks that have the potential to advance the things that we are trying to help, and the progress we're trying to help achieve.

In 2006, David Rockefeller, one of our founders, and I started having a set of conversations about what he could do to help the RBF. That led to an extraordinarily generous decision on his part that we will be receiving a significant bequest from him. We have been, with our Board of Trustees, engaged in a process, knowing that we would receive David's gift at some point in the future. We've been engaged in a multiyear process to think about how we can best utilize those resources.

We don't know exactly what the value of the bequest will be, because a lot of it is still in various assets that will need to be liquidated, but it will give us substantial additional capacity. It's both a wonderful opportunity and a welcome but heavy responsibility.

How can we best carry forward David Rockefeller's legacy? It comes with a great sense of sadness at his passing, but it is very exciting. It was just such a wonderful thing when he told me that he had made that decision. It was an incredible vote of confidence. We had our 75th anniversary in 2015, and David had been involved all 75 years. He was 25 when he and his brothers started the RBF, and because he was the youngest kid, they made him the recording secretary. If you look at the first board meeting minutes, they're all signed "David Rockefeller."

What is your organization doing internally and externally to address racial inequity?

I would say we are working on three dimensions. A few years back, we decided it was time to undertake a diagnostic look at our organizational culture, to figure out how healthy we were as an organization. We wanted to look at questions of diversity, equity and inclusion. That was a wake-up call, although we knew going in that there were issues. If you just look at the data, we do pretty well. We have a very diverse staff. We do particularly well on gender, like many nonprofit organizations. We are very diverse with regard to race and sexual preference and a variety of other factors. By the numbers, we were pretty good.

We did a deeper dive in this diagnostic work, and we found we were not as inclusive an organization as we thought we were or should be. That came through in confidential surveys and interviews conducted with staff at all levels of the organization by consultants, third parties who protected confidentiality. I was really surprised and concerned. So we started a process to try to engage staff in thinking about how we could become truly more inclusive. That's complicated work, and we have taken our temperature along the way. The more recent staff surveys suggest that we've made some good progress. But in the last year, the events in society around us, starting with the seemingly unending instances of police violence against people of color, put the issues in a different light.

After the Dallas shootings in 2016, I invited any staff members who wanted to to gather. I didn't have an agenda, and I didn't even really know what to say, except that I was very disturbed by what was happening in our society. I wanted this to be a place we could talk to each other about the state of racism in our society, and to think about what we might do.

It was hard for people to talk about this. One of my colleagues, who is African-American and a leader in the institution, said, "I'm not sure if this is a safe place for me to talk about how I feel about it." This again was hard news to hear, but exactly what you hope somebody will say, because only through honest interaction can we make progress together.

We are now in the next phase of an organizational-culture initiative we are inviting staff to help develop. We had some ideas we put on the table, and some seemed to resonate with staff and others didn't. We said, "Why don't those of you who are really interested in this or have some ideas or concerns get together, and then come back and tell us what you think would be the right way to broaden and deepen the conversation?" This is obviously not rocket science; it's harder than rocket science. But it's not something you do and move on. It's something you have to keep doing. It requires continuous attention.

What are we doing externally is the second part of your question. We are, of course, a nonpartisan organization, and we're very careful about that, but we are political in the sense that we believe that one of the most important acupuncture needles is to influence the exercise of public power. If you can influence public policy or private-sector behavior, you are really producing change, because those are the dominant sectors in our society. Those are our two primary areas of engagement.

Now we're in a policy environment very different from the one we've been operating under for the last eight years, and arguably for long before that. Many of our staff were shocked by the rhetoric and the outcome of the presidential election. We are a diverse organization, and a number of people on staff feel personally threatened by some of the policies of this administration. We have people who are green-card holders, people who are in the LGBTQ community, African-Americans, Latinos. People are worried—personally worried, even though they live in New York, which is a diverse and progressive city.

The three areas in which we work are strengthening the vitality of democracy, promoting sustainable development and building peace in the Middle East—in Israel, Palestine, U.S.-Iran relations and Afghanistan. All three of these areas are directly challenged by the policy directions of this new administration. We have spent the time since November preparing a plan for how RBF should position itself in the new environment.

I'm proud of the fact that the board has agreed to a 12 percent increase in our grant-making budget for the current year and probably for another two years, depending on how the market performs. This provides us more funding, especially to work on inclusive American democracy. Half of it will go into that portfolio, and half of it will go into a new fund that gives us the flexibility to respond to urgent needs that arise as a result of the initiatives of this administration.

The board has given us the flexibility to support initiatives that may be out of our usual areas of focus. But if they are urgent and need an infusion of capital, we have the means to act.

We have also decided that our values—institutional values about diversity and equity and inclusion—are going to be front and center. We will be looking to support organizations that are representative of marginalized and vulnerable communities as part of this initiative.

A 2016 U.S. Trust study shows that high net worth Americans have greater confidence in individuals and nonprofits than in the executive branch or Congress. With the current administration and Congress, what role should the nonprofit sector and organizations like yours play over the next several years?

That is an important question. The nonprofit sector is the guarantor of our democracy. The sector needs to acknowledge that more explicitly, and decide how at this moment we are going to collectively fulfill that responsibility. That's the conversation we need to have.

After the 2016 election, *The New York Times* reported, "the widening political divergence between cities and small-town America also reflects a growing alienation between the two groups, and a sense—perhaps accurate—that their fates are not connected." What role should the nonprofit sector play in helping the two groups find common ground?

Oddly enough, in the philanthropic world, we have focused our efforts on inclusion in a way that made a significant portion of the population of our country feel excluded. That is truly unfortunate. We know there are 1.7 million nonprofits in this country. Thousands and thousands of those organizations are in rural communities and in the middle of the country. Those are places to which the large foundations haven't been paying as much attention. So those organizations are a potential source of healing and progress, because they are part of this sector.

Inviting them to help educate us about life in the communities they serve, and what we might do differently, and do better to include those communities, can be an important part of the process. We have colleagues in all those communities and counties, and we need to invite them and listen to them and find ways to work together.

How are the choices of very wealthy private philanthropists influencing traditional foundation giving?

I've just started reading David Callahan's book, *The Givers: Wealth, Power, and Philanthropy in a New Gilded Age*. There is a lot of conversation about the new philanthropy versus the old philanthropy. I have not yet been persuaded there's that much difference between the two. There is one important difference, which is that the amount of new money is huge. The estimates of the generational transfer of wealth and the part that will end up going to philanthropic purposes adds up to tens of trillions of dollars in the decades ahead.

In a way, the new philanthropy—high-net-worth philanthropy—is going to become the dominant philanthropy. We have experienced this, in a modest way, at RBF. In the mid-1970s, the RBF was the 15th largest foundation in America. Today, we are the 93rd largest, measured by asset size. And it's not because we threw our money away or wasted it or spent it all down. It's because of all the additional wealth coming into philanthropy. It's changing the dynamics between foundations with a longer history, longer experience basis, multiple generations of leaders, and a lot of this new wealth that's coming in without that experience. Many are trying to invent a new operating system for philanthropy, which can be very exciting, but I don't think it's all that different yet. Some parts of what people consider the older, traditional philanthropy we are not about to throw out.

I encourage people to study the Rockefeller story. It's now a five-generation story. There is no other family in the world that has been as philanthropic for as many generations. They have been through a lot together. It wasn't always easy, but they worked it out. The lessons they learned will be valuable to this new wealth coming in. I will be interested to see how the wealth is organized, how the governance of these new foundations is established. I worry a little bit about the inequality aspect. All this wealth is a product of the enormous economic inequality in our society.

The first Rockefeller became unimaginably wealthy compared to the average citizen of his time. And he started out with nothing. We have in the archives his original ledger book from 1855, when he went to work at age 16. He made $45 that year. He gave away $5, so he was already giving away more than 10 percent. The wealth that is being created today is a product of economic inequality, and as a result, it sets up some challenging social and economic and even political dynamics. We may be getting to a point where we need to think about more oversight for private foundations. This will be very unpopular, and David Callahan's book has stirred controversy in this regard.

On one hand, one of our greatest assets is our independence. We don't want to lose our independence, because that gives us the ability to take risk. If the government sector and the private sector won't tackle a problem, foundations can step in. On the other hand, we need to do it in a transparent fashion. Right now, that is largely voluntary, and maybe some of that needs to become mandatory. That's the conversation we need to have as all this wealth makes its way into philanthropy and takes on big social issues.

If there were one thing you could say to your colleagues who are leading nonprofits seeking funding, what would it be?

Don't give up. Don't be discouraged by the unanswered email or the languishing proposal that's sitting on somebody's desk. That's actually more of a message to foundation staff. We need to be more responsive. It's hard, because we're working hard, reviewing a lot of proposals. A lot of people are asking for support. All are good ideas, but we need to work on improving our responsiveness. A quick "No" is a whole lot better than a long, long silence. The other thing I would say to them is study, because it will serve them well. It will make the nonprofit-foundation relationship more effective if grant-seekers really try to understand what foundations are interested in before they approach them.

Another responsibility for us is to communicate clearly what we're interested in, so that people will not spend a lot of time and energy, with limited resources, getting ready to send something we're not going to be able to support.

Since the best jokes have some truth behind them, what is your favorite joke about the nonprofit sector?

You've probably heard this from everybody you've had discussions with, but I remember the first time I heard it, when I was selected to come here. It goes like this: "When you come to work in philanthropy, you have just told your last bad joke and had your last bad meal." There's some truth to that. All of a sudden, you're a lot smarter than you used to be, and you're a lot funnier than you used to be.

CHAPTER 16

Hilary Pennington
Vice President, Ford Foundation

Hilary Pennington is vice president of the Ford Foundation's Education, Creativity and Free Expression program, leading the foundation's work on Youth Opportunity and Learning and Creativity and Free Expression. She oversees the BUILD initiative, a $1 billion investment to strengthen the core health and capabilities of grantee organizations around the world.

Additionally, she oversees the foundation's regional programming in four offices based in Africa and the Middle

East. Prior to joining Ford, Pennington held leadership positions at the Bill and Melinda Gates Foundation, the Center for American Progress and Jobs for the Future, which she co-founded. She also served on President Bill Clinton's transition team and as co-chair of his administration's presidential advisory committee on technology.

Pennington is a graduate of the Yale School of Management and Yale College. She holds a graduate degree in social anthropology from Oxford University and a master's of theological studies from the Episcopal Divinity School. She was a fellow at the Harvard Kennedy School of Government in 2000.

Ford Foundation

The Ford Foundation is an independent, nonprofit grant-making organization. For more than 80 years, it has worked with courageous people on the frontlines of social change worldwide, guided by its mission to strengthen democratic values, reduce poverty and injustice, promote international cooperation and advance human achievement. With headquarters in New York, the foundation has offices in Latin America, Africa, the Middle East and Asia.

Hilary Pennington

Who has had the greatest influence on you as a professional?

My mentor, Arthur White, who was a businessman and founded [the marketing and research firm] Yankelovich, Skelly & White. I started working with him when he was 60 and I was 28. We founded Jobs for the Future and worked really closely together while I was in that role for over 20 years. He remained a very influential mentor as I transitioned into working in philanthropy. He was unusual in that he saw potential in me as a young and untested person. He let me take on enormous responsibility and gave me credit and support in doing it.

From the beginning, he treated me as his equal when we met with corporate CEOs or with governors like Bill Clinton. He would structure the meetings and conversations so that I did half the talking. He was a big visionary who needed someone practical to help him realize those visions, so we had a unique partnership founded on deep respect. I was incredibly lucky to work with someone like that.

Thus far, what have been the worst and best events in your life, and what did those experiences teach you?

One of the worst was when I was 3 years old and my father died, leaving my mother with three children. I was the oldest, and my younger sister was born in the final months of my dad's life. She was born with a fairly serious cognitive disability. My mom was amazing. She never remarried, and she worked full-time, so she was unusual at that time as a single-mother professional, and she was a great role model.

My father's death changed our entire lives and my role in our family. Because of my sister, I have an acute sense of how much privilege you can have without earning it, and how different her life chances were from mine. That has been a big motivator for the kind of things I've worked on. The best thing that happened to me is a happy second marriage.

What, if anything, keeps you up at night?

The ways in which the norms of civility, empathy and tolerance that stitch societies together seem to be erod-ing all over the world, and how serious it is for cultures and societies when that happens. It's puzzling, because I think, in essence, it means that people in many places are saying, "This is too much change. I can't handle this anymore." And they're reverting to almost tribal ways of trying to deal with things. So how do you build back from there? How do you reignite the sense that what we have in common is greater than what divides us?

What is your definition of happiness, or, what is your philosophy of life?

My philosophy of life is to really live your life aspiring to make a positive impact. That requires working really hard to find joy and build trust in your personal and working relation-ships. If you hit a wall, you try to find the door in that wall, or make a door in that wall.

What would you say is the greatest misconception about you?

That I'm an extrovert. I have a warm energy and I like people, but I need a lot of down time for myself. I'm not the kind of person who gets recharged by being connected and on. I often get depleted. It's taken a long time to learn that and find the right balance.

What is the most important thing you tell young people who are thinking about making careers in the nonprofit sector?

I tell them to trust themselves and look for opportunities. It can really take time before you find the right path. You can often get better opportunities by being a big fish in a small pond, or working in a relatively smaller, less established organization, so don't be afraid to do that. Do what you're really passionate about, because that's how you're going to make the biggest impact.

What new opportunities do you see for Ford in the next five years?

Through our BUILD initiative, a $1 billion investment to strengthen the core health and capabilities of grantee organizations around the world, I see an opportunity to increase the effectiveness of key nonprofit sector organizations and to convince other funders that more patience and longer-term general support is the better way to go.

There are also a lot of opportunities to figure out how to work in the world at a time of closing space for civil society. That's both a challenge and an opportunity. The fields I focus on have to do with institutions of culture like journalism, arts and education. There's an opportunity to take what we're learning about developmental and learning science to improve the quality of supports for young people, and to transform education and people's experience of the arts so that they're more interactive. That will allow people to express and fulfill themselves more deeply.

We're in the midst of a national conversation about race and racial equity. What is your organization doing, both internally and externally, to address racial inequity?

Externally, it's the kinds of things we're funding. The largest programmatic grant-making area in the foundation is our Gender, Racial and Ethnic Justice program, which focuses on issues of structural discrimination. This includes our work on criminal justice reform, which is one of the most inequitable systems and structures in our society. Across all our programs, we are looking at how to approach our work in more intersectional ways.

As human beings, we are all more than one thing, so how do we think about coalitions that are built around the idea that *all* people should thrive and have their dignity recognized? In our education work, for example, we've decided to pivot away from institutional efforts like curriculum and teacher development and college access. We're focusing instead on holistic supports for the young people who are the most likely to experience inequality within big systems like education, immigration and juvenile justice.

Internally, we are doing a lot. We have a pretty intensive effort at diversity, equity and inclusion across multiple dimensions. Starting from the top, more than half of our board is made up of people of color and women. That's a big change from what it was before. We bring this same lens when it comes to recruiting staff at every level, and ensuring we have equity in compensation and leadership positions. And we ask the organizations we work with a lot of questions about their own commitment to diversity—this is true from the vendors we hire to the organizations we select for grants.

For example, our Creativity and Free Expression program prioritizes works of art and stories from people whose voices have typically been excluded. If you look at the composition of the decision-makers of media and cultural organizations, you'll see they haven't changed that much. Newsrooms are 90 percent white. Heads of museums are mostly white. A lack of diversity would be a serious setback in our consideration to give them a grant. In cases where we've made grants and we see an organization is not trying to make progress toward becoming more inclusive, we would eventually stop funding them.

After the 2016 election, *The New York Times* reported, "the widening political divergence between cities and small-town America also reflects a growing alienation between the two groups, and a sense—perhaps accurate—that their fates are not connected." What role should the nonprofit sector play in helping the two groups find common ground?

That sharpening our focus on what we're for, rather than what or who we're against, is one way to start. I'd start by reminding people of our common story. People have shared aspirations to have access to decent education, work, and health care for themselves and their children. There's a huge amount of regional dependence between cities and suburbs, even in the more rural areas. We should try to strengthen those links where they exist in a more intentional, physical way. It's important to disaggregate the data.

That's what so powerful about the work of Raj Chetty, the economist at Stanford University. His data is broken down by counties, cities, ZIP codes and neighborhoods across the United States. You can see which regions promote mobility from the bottom to the top. For example, there are places where some things happen and places where they don't. You can see why one side of Cleveland is more effective at doing something than the other side. We need to think with less generality and learn more about real particulars and what's happening to the mobility in specific places. It's the particularity of Chetty's data that's so powerful, so we're helping to fund the research, and we'll definitely use that data.

How would you say the choices of the very wealthy, private philanthropists are influencing traditional foundation giving, if at all?

The advent of new philanthropists is causing traditional philanthropy to think about how we can partner. Often new philanthropists have particular passions, a set of beliefs about how change happens, and a lot of confidence in that because of their experience. I think many of them start in philanthropy with a lot of enthusiasm for particular kinds of interventions, whether it's some sort of technology, intervention or model. They have a very constructive urgency about impact and scaling.

Because they tend to focus so much there, it allows philanthropies like ours to focus more on a complementary set of things that have to do more with the root causes. What is it about the rules of the game, power dynamics, underlying beliefs and narratives that keep inequalities in place? For example, at the Ford Foundation, we're supporting efforts that drive social change, like building strong coalitions and networks, investing in grassroots organizing and promoting more inclusive narratives. We are able to do this, in part, because there are so many resources from other funders going toward systems change and testing or scaling new models.

Many of the new entrants are still learning about the combination of evidence, politics, social change, and what it means to get something from one place to many. Sometimes it's more of a question of public will than it is about whether a model or particular solution is effective or not. The presence of evidence alone doesn't mean a particular solution will be adopted or used in a way that has a lasting change. That's why it's a good moment for partnership among newer and older philanthropies, because you always need proof points and models, but you also need to pay attention to the power dynamics in a democratic society that cause those things to become expected practices.

CHAPTER 17

Build Broad-Based Coalitions

In addition to campaigning on many fronts, it is critical, in social change-making, to build broad-based coalitions of different types of constituencies. Campaigning and building coalitions go together, and it is difficult to separate one from the other, but we have isolated the two issues to illustrate the many elements that go into making positive social change.

Here are some things to think about when you are building coalitions.

A. Seek Strategic Partnerships; Learn from Successful Movements

Tara Perry is CEO of the national association of Court Appointed Special Advocates (CASA), which supports and promotes court-appointed advocates for abused or neglected children. She says, "One of the things this sector has struggled with is collaboration. If it were easy, people would do it. We could start to approach things the way the corporate world does it, by merging or acquiring. The sector has to think about how you can partner, how you can joint-venture, in ways that take away the [perceived] threat [of competition], to grow and be stronger together."

One organization that is taking collaboration seriously is WNET, the parent company of Channel 13 in New York City. WNET has begun to reach out to nonprofits and community groups to help them tell their stories. Neal Shapiro, the public television station's president and CEO, says, "We [recently] started something called *Parenting Minutes*. The premise is to work with people in diverse neighborhoods. We are doing short videos on how you can help your family. One video is about what to do with lead-based paint. Another is about how to encourage your kid not to drink so much soda. A third is about healthy snacks. The key is that we do the videos in the three most common languages in New York, in addition to English: Spanish, Chinese and Bengali."

Organizations often need to be cajoled or even pressed into partnerships. A lack of resources is one issue. Managing partnerships takes time. Unless there is a person on staff whose job it is to lead them, partnerships are unlikely to become a priority for your organization.

Because of her 50,000-foot view of the sector, Stacy Palmer, editor of the *Chronicle of Philanthropy,* is particularly knowledgeable about macro trends. She says, "Nonprofits need to collaborate more and stop competing with each other as much as they do."

This is a Catch-22 for many small organizations. Their leaders know they can make a bigger impact if they partner, but they just don't have the resources to do it effectively and deliver their core programs at the same time.

This brings us to one of our strong beliefs. The nation has too many nonprofits. Staff and board members may insist that the mission and programs of their organization are unique, but that is simply not true. For proof, check online for the "Top 100 mission statements."

Small organizations and start-ups are innovative and nimble, playing an important role in advancing the nonprofit sector as a whole. They would be better positioned to sustain their work if they considered mergers or other forms of alliances with larger nonprofits as strategic choices, rather than last-ditch efforts to survive.

In spring 2014, the *Stanford Social Innovation Review* published an article[12] on nonprofit mergers and acquisitions called "Why Nonprofit Mergers Continue to Lag." The obstacles they point to—creating alignment within the boards, finding roles for senior staff and blending the brands—square with our experience of nonprofit mergers, both successful and attempted.

When one of us was a vice president at a good-sized nonprofit about a decade ago, our visionary CEO conceived the idea of merging with an organization that had complementary geography and a very similar program. The negotiations advanced quite far. We put together binders with information on each organization. Our CEO and board chair

---

12   Katie Smith Milway, Maria Orozco and Cristina Botero: "Why Nonprofit Mergers Continue to Lag," *Stanford Social Innovation Review*, Spring 2014. https://ssir.org/articles/entry/why_nonprofit_mergers_continue_to_lag.

had closed-door talks with various leaders at the other organization. Then, the other board voted the merger down because many of its volunteers had expressed their opposition to it.

We do not know if that merger could have happened under different circumstances. What we do know is that the other board did not have a clear enough vision of what the combined organization could achieve.

At least one of our interviewees agrees with our assessment. Since we interviewed him, Tom Dente of InsideNGO has merged his organization with two other organizations serving the international development community. The new organization, Humentum, will serve development, humanitarian, civil society and other international nonprofit sector organizations, with a focus on supporting operational excellence. He says he has been getting inquiries from other leaders about mergers. This is a hopeful sign.

A striking summary of the issues facing nonprofits, and in fact, society as a whole, comes from Henry Timms of 92Y, which "promotes individual and family development and participation in civic life within the context of Jewish values and American pluralism."[13] In late 2014, Timms and Jeremy Heimans wrote a piece for the *Harvard Business Review* called "Understanding New Power."[14] They see the emergence of two unexpected forces as the structures of the 20th century shift and in some cases disintegrate. They see strongmen

---

13   92Y.org, "About Us." https://www.92y.org/mission-history (accessed August 6, 2017).
14   Heimans, Jeremy and Henry Timms: "Understanding New Power," *Harvard Business Review*, December 2014. https://hbr.org/2014/12/understanding-new-power.

taking over in many countries (old power), and they see platforms, often digital, making it easier for people to exercise power through sharing, shaping, funding, producing and co-owning content and policy (new power). One power is handed down from the top; the other flows, like electricity.

The challenge for nonprofits, particularly venerable ones, is to retain some institutional structure (old power), while enabling people to engage in meaningful ways on their own terms (new power). The key is to mobilize people around issues they care about in ways that benefit society, while nurturing the expertise that makes it possible to identify and understand those issues.

Black Lives Matter is the network most often cited by our leaders as succeeding brilliantly by utilizing new power. When it burst onto the scene in 2013, after an African-American teenager, Trayvon Martin, was shot by a neighborhood watch volunteer in a suburb in Florida, foundations and others did not really know how to support it, because it was a movement, not a single organization. Of course, Black Lives Matter has since gotten a fiscal sponsor, an organization that can accept donations for it. And people have made many, many contributions to it. In 2016, the Ford Foundation and the Borealis Fund got together with other donors to pledge $100 million over six years to the movement through an African-American-led Movement Fund.

We do not know what the consequences of this will be for the nonprofit sector. No one really does. Our hypothesis is that, as with natural selection, some venerable institutions will adapt and survive, while others will die or become irrelevant.

We can see this tension playing out at the Metropolitan Museum of Art, the country's largest art museum. Thomas Campbell, who had been CEO of the museum for eight years, resigned in February 2017 after concerns about the museum's financial health.

Campbell brought the Met into the 21st century by creating a digital department and staging some wonderful exhibits featuring artists of color. You can now see and share many of the objects in the Met's collection online—trying to answer the call of the public for new power. But most of the art is still not relevant to the vast majority of visitors—a remnant of old power.

The Met will survive, as it has a number of times through difficult periods. But it may look and feel very different when its transformation, and that of many other museums around the country, is complete.

B. Leverage Your Convening Influence

Fred Blackwell at the San Francisco Foundation understands that the foundation must seek partnerships to accomplish its 10-year goal: to increase racial equity and inclusion in the Bay Area against the backdrop of the highest real estate prices in the country. Blackwell says the foundation is talking to donors and leveraging its reputation and grant-making to step into a more public role. "There are many people in the Bay Area who have been working on this for years on the ground, but they've been operating without an adequate amount of support and cover from the public sector. … We want to use our influence to bring a new set of players to the table and hopefully tap into the passions and interests of Bay Area philanthropists so they'll want to join us in addressing equity in the Bay Area."

Media outlets, like WNET, have more convening power than other nonprofits. Laura Walker, president of WNYC, the New York City National Public Radio affiliate, is committed to working across the urban-rural divide that became so apparent after the 2016 election. Walker says, "Right after the election, we asked ourselves around the table: "What can we do to bridge the divide?" It was the urban-rural divide, but also the red and blue divide and many other divides. One of the things we did was to start a national talk show." She reached out to her colleagues in Minnesota, and together they created a show called "Indivisible," which they describe as "public radio's national conversation about America in a time of change."[15]

Foundations definitely have an edge over public charities in convening because of their grant-making power. However, just as nonprofits underestimate their advocacy power, they also underestimate their convening power.

C. Include Communities of Faith

We learned through our research that nonprofits and foundations are beginning to recognize the importance of including communities of faith in making social change. Nowhere is this inclusion more important than in bridging the urban-rural divide. That divide has existed in this

---

15   WNYC, "About Indivisible." http://www.wnyc.org/shows/indivisible/about (accessed August 8, 2017).

country for a long time, but became painfully evident after the 2016 election.

In rural communities, churches and other places of worship are often the most prominent representatives of social welfare, from their soup kitchens and homeless shelters to resettling refugees.

We asked how nonprofits could help find common ground between the urban and rural divide. Brian McLaren, a prominent Christian activist and author, says, "We're all fragmented into very small interest groups, like urban versus rural people, or professionals versus blue-collar workers. Every time you sit down to a meal, however, the truth is that all those sectors are brought together because a farmer and farmworker grew and harvested the food that we eat."

McLaren continues, "Getting a bigger picture and acknowledging that human beings and their well-being count seems to be an important part of social entrepreneurship. You could easily sell a fair-trade shirt, and it would mean workers get fair wages, and the dyes used were not harmful to the environment, but the buyers might not even know it's a fair-trade shirt. It would be great if we could raise people's consciousness of their connection to each other through every economic transaction."

The Katharine Katharine R. Henderson is president of Auburn Seminary, which "equips leaders with the organizational skills and spiritual resilience required to create lasting, positive impact in local communities, on the national stage, and around the world."[16] Auburn's work is training religious leaders to make positive social change. Henderson says, "I think the opportunity now is to create new partnerships. There is a lot of porousness. Some of the divides that have separated us, such as faith-based and secular, are changing. That is really important. We must work together. I'm very interested in a new opportunity where Muslims and Jews are working together in new ways, beyond Muslims and Jews and Christians and Sikhs."

D. Fund-Raise Aggressively

Just as you needed seed money to get started, you will need bigger money to expand your solution. This will be much easier if you have proven your concept through a pilot program and can talk confidently about its impact.

The nonprofit leaders we interviewed want more foundation funding for unrestricted support. Unrestricted support is an expression of trust in the nonprofit to use the money in a way that achieves the greatest leverage for its mission. We heard this over and over again in different ways—and we have been hearing the same thing from organizations for 20 years.

Hilary Pennington is vice president for education, creativity and free expression at the Ford Foundation. We asked her what opportunities she sees for the foundation over the next five years, and the first thing she said was, "Through our BUILD initiative, a $1 billion investment to strengthen the

---

core health and capabilities of grantee organizations around the world, I see an opportunity to increase the effectiveness of key nonprofit sector organizations and to convince other funders that more patience and longer-term general support is the better way to go." If Ford, one of the most influential foundations in the world, is spending $1 billion on this kind of initiative, it is our bet that other funders will follow suit before too long.

A related concern is foundations funding only the incremental costs of programs, rather than the full cost. Tom Dente says, "Let's move away from those artificial labels and just talk about what are the true costs of getting the results we want. Let's fund full cost where we can, so we achieve the results we desire. Let's not be guided by dated, old-fashioned accounting metrics, but by impact."

That it could be wrong to fund the full cost of a program has always struck us as strange. We have been in many, many meetings where we twisted ourselves and our financial data into knots to make it look as if a program cost less than it actually did. We knew the traditional foundation model was to fund a lot of organizations with a little money for each one. Now, with the trend developing of foundations funding fewer organizations with larger amounts of money, nonprofits have no excuse not to ask for the full cost—and keep asking until they get it!

Paula Kerger, CEO of the Public Broadcasting System (PBS), makes the plea that foundations encourage nonprofits to take risks and then support them if they fail. We heard this request that foundations behave more like investors from several different interviewees. Allowing a nonprofit to take a risk requires a high degree of trust between the nonprofit and the foundation program officer. A high level of trust requires an open and honest relationship, which takes time and attention to build.

We also asked about the dynamic between traditional foundations, such as Ford, and new philanthropists such as Mark Zuckerberg of Facebook.

Jane O'Connell, CEO of the Altman Foundation, told us, "I think in some ways they've been an enormously good influence. They have taken stands on things and picked issues that are really important, that I think have highlighted how you can really make change by putting a lot of force, money and influence behind it. I think they have opened up people's minds to what philanthropy can do."

Stephen Heintz of the Rockefeller Brothers Fund, says, "I encourage people to study the Rockefeller story. It's now a five-generation story. There is no other family in the world that has been as philanthropic for as many generations. They have been through a lot together. It wasn't always easy, but they worked it out. The lessons they learned will be valuable to this new wealth coming in."

Fred Blackwell of the San Francisco Foundation agrees, but also thinks those engaged in more traditional philanthropy could learn from the new philanthropists. He says, "We should be aiming for a sweet spot" between the energy of the new philanthropists and the long experience of traditional philanthropists.

New philanthropists bring much-needed capital to the sector. They come with good intentions. They want to make a difference in the world, and the world needs them.

Gali Cooks is the founding executive director of the Leading Edge, which "addresses the root causes that prevent Jewish nonprofits from having the outstanding leaders they need."[17] Cooks says, "Foundations should be acting more like major capitalists. That's really part of the way that we're going to move society forward. It's not only funding the museum, but asking what the museum does to make us better or think differently. Younger funders have a certain level of impatience, and they are not going to accept the answer of 'This is how it has always been done.'"

We encourage nonprofit executives to select the foundations they believe could be most helpful to them in the long run. We recommend allocating the time to invest in the relationship, even if it is several years before any money changes hands. The organizations that do this rarely regret it.

---

17   Leading Edge, "What We Do." http://leadingedge.org/#front-page-2 (accessed August 8, 2017).

CHAPTER 18

Brian McLaren

Co-Founder, The Convergence
Leadership Project

Brian D. McLaren is an author, speaker, activist and public theologian. A former college English teacher and pastor, he is a passionate advocate for "a new kind of Christianity": just, generous and working with people of all faiths for the common good. He is an Auburn senior fellow and a leader in the Convergence Network, through which he is developing an innovative training/mentoring program for pastors, church planners and lay leaders called the Convergence Leadership Project.

Born in 1956, he graduated from the University of Maryland with B.A. and master's degrees in English. His academic interests included medieval drama, the Romantic poets, modern philosophical literature and the novels of Dr. Walker Percy. In 2004, he was awarded a doctor of divinity degree from Carey Theological Seminary in Vancouver, British Columbia, and in 2010, he received a second honorary doctorate, from Virginia Theological Seminary (Episcopal).

McLaren has been active in networking and mentoring church planners and pastors since the mid-1980s, and has assisted in the development of several new churches. He is a popular conference speaker and a frequent guest lecturer for denominational and ecumenical leadership gatherings across the United States and Canada, Latin America, Europe, Africa and Asia. His public speaking covers a broad range of topics, including postmodern thought and culture, Biblical studies, evangelism, leadership, global mission, spiritual formation, worship, pastoral survival and burnout, inter-religious dialogue, ecology and social justice.

The Convergence Leadership Project

The Convergence Leadership Project aims to equip church leaders, clergy and lay, to become vibrant spiritual activists in a growing, multi-denominational movement of just, generous and joyful Christianity. Many churches and denominations, like the United States at large, are polarized and paralyzed. They have to walk on eggshells for fear of offending members (including major donors) who openly or tacitly support an ugly, fearful resurgence of white Christian nationalism. The Convergence Leadership Project is helping progressive Christians and congregations find each other, dream together and learn, get organized and work together for the common good.

Brian McLaren

Who has had the greatest influence on you as a professional?

There have been so many. I've been deeply influenced by a Catholic novelist named Walker Percy. His writing in the 1970s had a big effect on me in the area of social change and justice. Another great influence has been an economist named Herman Daly, who was one of the first economists to say that when you make a profit by destroying the environment, that's not actually a profit. Then there's a former pastor named John Maxwell, who did a great job introducing people in the religious world to leadership theory. Clergy, in many ways, were trained as scholars, and leadership was secondary for them, but John started talking to them about leadership as the most important part of their job.

Thus far, what have been the worst and best events in your life, and what did those experiences teach you?

The worst was when one of my four children was diagnosed with leukemia at the age of 6. He went through three and a half years of chemotherapy, and came through great. It was a great outcome, but a rough couple of years. In some ways, it was the worst and best thing together. I was in my early 30s, working way too hard, and when my son got sick, I realized I don't have any time to waste on secondary things. I think that had a big role in teaching me how to prioritize and distinguish the urgent from the truly important.

What, if anything, keeps you up at night?

The area where I feel a sense of calling is in trying to help religious communities be a force for good and progress in the world, instead of a force for evil and regression. We're going through a global civilizational shift in so many different areas, including faith, spirituality and religion. In times of turbulence like this, it's natural that there will be regressive forces that make people want to retreat into the past, cling to the familiar, and lean backwards into nostalgic fantasies about some idealized golden age. What keeps me up at night is that we need a spiritual vision of the future, and we need to build a progressive faith movement within each religious tradition and then among them together.

What is your definition of happiness, or, what is your philosophy of life?

I believe at the core of all of our faiths and traditions is one primary teaching, and that is that we're all connected and we need to act like it. So, helping people discover and live in light of their connection is a great challenge to me, and I think that sense of connection is still under threat today. I try to discipline my own inner life and my behavior to contribute rather than take away from the large community I'm part of.

A mentor of mine taught me a poem:

I slept and dreamed that life was joy
I woke and saw that life was service
And then I served, so now I know:
Service is joy.

It's a beautiful poem, and I think that entering into that connectedness can bring great pain; but it also brings life's greatest joy.

What is the greatest misconception about you?

I have a lot of critics in the more conservative, religious world, and I think their main misconception is that to be faithful, you have to be conservative. So to be creative or progressive isn't an act of infidelity to the tradition; it's actually an act of deep fidelity. It's loving the tradition enough to help it keep growing, adapting and being fruitful in new historical and cultural contexts.

What is the most important thing you tell young people who are thinking about making careers in the nonprofit sector?

I try to tell them three things. One is discover your passion and follow it. The second is to take care of yourself, because so many people who are motivated by passion end up burning out if they're not doing the right kind of self-care. The third is to think long-term, because even though it's true that life is short, it's also true that life is long. We often get wrapped up in that one project or one emergency that we're facing now, and we have to keep stepping back and getting the long view.

What new opportunities do you see for your organizations?

I'm the chairman of the board of two closely related organizations, Convergence and the Center for Progressive

Renewal. The recent election has pulled the curtain back on some realities that we thought were behind us, but we realized they're still here. The sense that things are worse than we thought creates an opportunity to shake the people who have been somewhat apathetic or complacent, and make them see they can't just celebrate that other people are doing the work. It's an "All hands on deck" moment, and everyone's engagement is needed. These organizations are trying to help mobilize progressive Christian communities throughout different denominations and congregations, to align their efforts and increase their effectiveness together.

We are in the midst of a national conversation about race and racial equity. What are your organizations doing both internally and externally to address racial inequity?

One of the things the Center for Progressive Renewal does is offer online training about white privilege, racial equality and anti-racism. One of the things I'm committed to is helping people see the theological roots of racism, and that racism often flows from misguided theology. In the fourth century, the idea of original sin was adopted. The idea that God has this wrath against everyone except for a chosen few is fertile ground for hostility toward others, if you see yourself as one of the chosen few insiders. I think that belief will continue to cause various forms of hostility until the Christian community disarms it.

If we deal with this theological hostility at the root, we can challenge people on the level of beliefs and world views, so their behavior can change for the better. You can't just take a harmful belief away from people. You have to replace it with a better belief, a better vision. That's why I try, in my writing and speaking, to give people a better way of reading the Bible and interpreting Christian history.

After the 2016 election, *The New York Times* reported, "the widening political divergence between cities and small-town America also reflects a growing alienation between the two groups, and a sense—perhaps accurate—that their fates are not connected." What role should the nonprofit sector play in helping the two groups find common ground?

This comes back to what I was saying about connection. We're all fragmented into very small interest groups, like urban versus rural people, or professionals versus blue-collar workers. Every time you sit down to a meal, however, the truth is that all those sectors are brought together because a farmer and farmworker grew and harvested the food that we eat. That means the most elite urban dweller is connected by everything he eats to his rural neighbor. We don't have anybody reminding us of these stories of connection. We buy a piece of chicken wrapped in plastic and Styrofoam, and we might go for 20 years without even thinking that that chicken was raised somewhere and that there were people involved.

The challenge to me is helping people understand that our interests are intertwined. This is important work in the nonprofit sector, and I think we can accomplish that by helping people understand that our self-interest is connected to the well-being of others. I also think the development of empathy, compassion and concern for your neighbor is something the nonprofit sector can and should be working on.

This is part of what's going on right now with our economic crisis. People read abstract numbers when measuring economics, but they're only measuring profits. They're not measuring well-being, so they are not understanding that corporate profits can go up while millions of people are shoved into unemployment. Getting a bigger picture and acknowledging that human beings and their well-being count seems to be an important part of social entrepreneurship.

You could easily sell a fair-trade shirt, and it would mean workers get fair wages, and the dyes used were not harmful to the environment, but the buyers might not even know that it's a fair-trade shirt. All they know is that they're paying for a shirt. But if by buying that shirt, they can also be bonding with whoever produced it, then we can increase a sense of connection. It would be great if we could raise people's consciousness of their connection to each other, through every economic transaction.

If there were one thing you could say to your colleagues who are leading grant-making foundations, what would it be?

I would say most grant-making organizations that I've had to deal with have a strong bias toward investing in existing institutions. I understand why that's the case, but in times of radical change, we need to invest in creative entrepreneurs who are at the front end of creating new institutions. I would urge them not to forget those highly creative entrepreneurial people who might seem like a higher risk. There are results we'll never get through incremental institutional improvements. There's progress that is only going to be made through a kind of venture capital for new ideas.

I would also say to find young leaders with great potential, creativity and engagement. They are a resource in and of themselves. There's no substitute for helping some of these leaders at the right time, and if grant-makers can find ways to lift the confidence, support and training of some of these young people, that would be remarkable.

CHAPTER 19

Teresa C. Younger

President and CEO, Ms. Foundation for Women

Teresa C. Younger has served as president and CEO of the Ms. Foundation for Women, the oldest women's foundation in the United States, since 2014. Under her leadership, the Foundation launched #MyFeminismIs, a multimedia campaign sparking a national conversation on feminism; funded a ground-breaking report on the sexual abuse to prison pipeline; joined leading women's foundations at the White House to announce a $100 million funding commitment to create pathways to economic opportunity for low-income women and girls; and led a campaign to hold the NFL accountable for violence against women.

A noted speaker, advocate, and activist, Younger has been on the frontlines of some of the most important battles for women's health, safety and economic justice. She was honored by Planned Parenthood Federation of America as a Dream Keeper, given Liberty Bank's Willard M. McRae Community Diversity Award and named one of the 50 Most Powerful Women in Philanthropy by Inside Philanthropy. A graduate of the University of North Dakota, Younger currently serves on the board of several philanthropic and advocacy organizations and initiatives, including: Grantmakers for Girls of Color (G4GC), Black Funders for Social Justice, the ERA Coalition, ACLU Awards Committee (2017), Essie Justice Project (board member), Funders for Reproductive Equity (FRE) (board member) and Philanthropy New York (board member).

In addition, she serves on boards or committees for the Ethel Walker School, the Women's Building, Women's Campaign School at Yale and the New York State Council on Women and Girls.

Foundation

The Foundation starts with the knowledge that the fight is not yet over. Although it is true that women have come a long way since the 1970s, for every woman who has reached the top, millions of women are struggling to earn a living wage, gain access to basic health care, to secure affordable child care and to participate in the opportunities that should be available to every person in the United States.

The Foundation is working to bring attention to the real challenges facing women, especially women of color and low-income women who are living in poverty, working paycheck to paycheck or both. It tirelessly advocates for national and statewide policy change that will address these challenges, and supports more than 100 organizations throughout the country that are working for change on a grassroots level.

Teresa C. Younger

Who has had the greatest influence on you as a professional?

One person is Carla Harris, who wrote a book called *Expect to Win*, which has had a profound impact on how I have thought about advancing myself, promoting my career and doing what I think needs to be done. The other person is a private day camp director I worked with over 20 years ago, Jeff Ackerman. He saw something in me I had not seen and put me on the course to where I am today.

Thus far, what have been the worst and best events in your life, and what did those experiences teach you?

One of the most impactful things that happened was when I quit college to be a nanny. I'm a first-generation college student, so it was one of those moments where I took a risk. There was a sign in the university library that said, "Nanny needed in Connecticut." I was attending the University of North Dakota, where I had grown up. I took the sign, called the woman on the paper, quit college for two years and became a nanny, much to my parents' surprise and chagrin.

I spent two amazing years working for a family with three little girls, who gave me the opportunity to volunteer time at an inner-city youth center and to work with more privileged students than the ones I had grown up with. It was also impactful because it helped me recommit myself to going back to college. I recognized what I needed to do to get the job done and get out of college. I wanted to change the lives of children and have an impact on the world, but I ended up getting a degree in recreation and leisure services. It's an unusual degree when most people see where I am now with the Ms. Foundation for Women. Part of the reason I got it was because when I looked over everything I needed to graduate, this was what gave me the greatest impact to be able to work in the nonprofit sector.

What, if anything, is keeping you up at night?

I'm an Air Force brat. My father was in the military for over 20 years, so I spent all my childhood moving around. I developed an appreciation for the service that men and women in this country give. What keeps me up at night is the lack of understanding about the role of government in the lives of people, and our obligation and commitment to creating a better world. I spend a lot of time, particularly under this administration, perplexed about what role I can play in generating respect for and preservation of democracy.

What is your definition of happiness, or, what is your philosophy of life?

My philosophy of life is to leave the world a better place than you found it. I grew up as a Girl Scout, so I am a lifetime member of the Girl Scouts. They believe in respecting people and making the world a better place, so that is so ingrained in who I am. My definition of happiness is hiking on a mountain on a beautiful spring day.

What is the greatest misconception about you?

Maybe that I'm intense. I really like to have a lot of fun, but I think I come off as intense, because I'm really driven to make sure we get things done.

What is the most important thing you tell young people who are thinking about making careers in the nonprofit sector?

I tell people to take risks, and if you don't get there, take another risk and do other things to get where you want to be. You wouldn't assume that being a nanny and running a children's residential camp would get me to where I am today, but all of those experiences have built on themselves. Sometimes young people think they're just going to end up where they want to be in life, but I would say that the road is not straight. It has lots of curves and right angles, and you should take advantage of both.

What new opportunities do you see for your organization in the next five years?

We're going through a strategic planning process right now. One of the things that will be critical over the next five years will be opening and expanding a conversation to build on collective power. When I say that, I'm talking about looking at cross-movement building and issues that are affecting the lives of women, not just the concept of women's issues. For me, it's a question of using terminology that brings more people to the table. How do we challenge the way we are thinking? In some ways, I hope what comes out of our strategic planning process is a commitment to continue to challenge the narrative that is most inclusive.

We have men on our board here, but I'm looking to expand it by a few more men as a national foundation, because I think it matters who carries your message. If we're talking about full equality for all genders, then we need to acknowledge that women really do not get full levels of equality until men also get full levels of equality. There are men in this country who only know a world where women have the same access that men have—or at least the same perceived access. We need to have that diversity and inclusion at all levels.

We are in the midst of a national conversation about race and racial equity. What is your organization doing, both internally and externally, to address racial inequity?

At the Foundation, we have always centered on the voices of the most marginalized community that holds the greatest level of power, but never gets heard. We've centered on women of color in our conversation and in the work we do, and how we fund in that space. Our staff is now 70 percent women of color, and our grantees are 65 percent women of color. One-third of our board is made up of people of color. One of the things I'm very intentional about is making sure we live the value that we talk about, and that we understand what that needs to look like. For me, as a woman of color, that means stepping in and being in those spaces that we might not have otherwise been in.

A 2016 U.S. Trust study shows that high net worth Americans have greater confidence in individuals and nonprofits than in the executive branch or Congress. With the current administration and Congress, what role

should the nonprofit sector and organizations like yours play over the next several years?

We have an obligation to reinforce the role of government. It goes back to my concern for the lack of understanding about the role of government. I'm not just talking about the national side, but what's happening in city councils, on the boards of education in their county governments and in their state governments. If we were to ask these questions, it would make it much more personal. When organizations like mine fund grantees and support their level of policy work, it helps reinforce the idea that we can't do this by ourselves. It's not necessarily the role of philanthropy to save government. It's up to all of us—nonprofits, individuals, philanthropists and the government.

After the 2016 election, *The New York Times* reported, "the widening political divergence between cities and small-town America also reflects a growing alienation between the two groups, and a sense—perhaps accurate—that their fates are not connected." What role should the nonprofit sector play in helping the two groups find common ground?

I often laugh at the fact that I grew up in North Dakota and am now living in an urban environment that is not reflective of where I grew up. Urban environments had to get filled by somebody, and many of those people come from rural communities. I think there just need to be more opportunities for integrated conversations to take place. In many ways, we have become disconnected, so we need to have a serious conversation about rebuilding that relationship.

What we saw in this election was a true disconnect in the values we have in this country and how we want to build on them. I think a key role would be to fund cross-sector convening and opportunities to bring those worlds together, and to be very conscious about what's happening in the rest of the country, when we live on the coast. I think we have to be conscious about how we talk about rural communities, because language is important, and there's been a real tearing down of how much we respect who lives where, and I don't think that's fair.

I think the Women's March in Washington and the movement we saw in so many places around the country helped us to see that we're not so far apart in some ways. I had friends who weren't activists before organizing in their small towns, even if it was 30 people getting together at a coffee shop because it was too cold to go outside. It reflected a level of values and priorities that we shared, in a way that was really wonderful.

We need to fund more studies so that we can act in those communities and speak to the shared values, as opposed to just policy or the other components we try to address.

If there were one thing you could say to your colleagues who are leading grant-making foundations, what would it be?

Trust women and take a risk. Take a moment to stop looking at shiny objects. Sometimes we look to the shiny object to find the answer, but it's really organizations like the Foundation or intermediaries that can help get to the ground faster. Trust that women have the answer to help and heal their communities. We have to trust them to come up with those and take the risk. Seven percent of philanthropic dollars go to women and young girls, and even less than that goes to women and girls of color. There needs to be a significant increase in supporting women's leadership and the issues that are identified by women. Many of the greatest thinkers are women leading small nonprofits, who are more worried about turning their lights on than trying to resolve the problem. In the philanthropic sector, we have helped suppress the nonprofit sector salaries by not doing multi-year grant-making and not providing general operating support.

How important is it to find the right people for your board, and what qualities do you look for? How successful have you been in matching those qualities?

It's incredibly important to find the right board members. The only person in my line of work that reports to a board is the CEO. Making sure that you have the right team to support and challenge you is really critical. We've done reasonably well in the past few years that I've been here, and I think even before that, at identifying the skill sets and overall diversity that we are seeking on our board to really round it out. The board has been receptive to our ongoing conversations about race and gender diversity.

I always say if we could have a pool of 20 individuals who cared not only about the Foundation, but cared more broadly about the social justice movement, we'd be right on target. We probably have a bench of about five to 10 right now, so we're just a few people short. Our eyes are constantly open. Last year, we expanded our board size so that we could achieve diversity in terms of skills and geography. As a national board, we really look across the country to make sure we have representation all over the place. You have to have a strategy, so my board is about 70 percent new board members from the last two and a half years. Part of that is due to the natural rolling term, but also because we've been identifying what we're looking for and bringing on new members. I think CEOs rarely recognize that a board takes true board management and time.

For us, it's been about knowing who we have and doing our board matrix, and then being intentional about developing a relationship. There are people who are great connectors, and I can go to them and say I'm looking for board members who have the capacity to give. It's also about being blunt. I may love a certain person, but I don't need another white woman on my board. Be honest about what you're looking to do. You have to figure out how to engage other people in different ways. I could easily build my board with people from New York and D.C., but that wouldn't reflect the diversity I'm trying to achieve.

What is the biggest lesson you've ever learned in hiring or letting people go?

They always say hire slowly and fire quickly, and I think I've had to fire many in my time at the ACLU, the Women's Commission and at the Foundation. A transition does not have to be all bad if you keep an open conversation and relationship through the process. I learned from one of my mentors, Jeff Ackerman, who used to fire people, and they would leave saying, "Thank you." I want to be compassionate in my firing, yet clear that it needs to happen.

How has your organization successfully scaled up its program?

By being intentional, listening and operating in a collaborative way.

What's your favorite book and why?

One of my favorite books most recently is Gloria Steinem's *My Life on the Road*. She released it right as I was coming off my listening tour [a trip across the country to meet with Foundation constituents]. I was able to travel across the country and be in conversation with her. She often said, "Because I was willing to just stop and listen, there tended to be a great connection." What she does really well is listen and develop relationships.

The best jokes have some truth behind them. What is your favorite joke about your profession or the nonprofit sector?

It's more of a saying than a joke, but it keeps me giggling at the end of the day. "The dream is free. The hustle is sold separately." It's so true.

CHAPTER 20

Fred Blackwell

CEO, San Francisco Foundation

Fred Blackwell is the CEO of the San Francisco Foundation, one of the largest community foundations in the country. San Francisco Foundation works with donors, community leaders and both public and private partners to create thriving communities throughout the Bay Area. Since joining the foundation in 2014, he has led the foundation in a renewed commitment to social justice through an equity agenda focused on racial and economic inclusion.

Blackwell, an Oakland native, is a recognized community leader with a long-standing career in the Bay Area. Before joining the foundation, he served as interim city administrator for the City of Oakland, where he had served as assistant city administrator. He was the executive director of the San Francisco Redevelopment Agency and director of the Mayor's Office of Community Development in San Francisco. He served as the director of the Making Connections Initiative for the Annie E. Casey Foundation in the lower San Antonio neighborhood of Oakland; and was a multicultural fellow at the San Francisco Foundation.

He currently serves on the board of the Independent Sector, Northern California Grantmakers, SPUR, the Bridgespan Group, the dean's advisory council for the University of California at Berkeley's College of Environmental Design, and the community advisory council of the San Francisco Federal Reserve. He is a visiting professor in the UC Berkeley Department of City and Regional Planning, and the co-chair of CASA (the Committee to House the Bay Area). He holds a master's degree in city planning from UC Berkeley and a bachelor's degree in urban studies from Morehouse College.

The San Francisco Foundation

With more than $1.3 billion in assets, the San Francisco Foundation is one of the largest community foundations in the country. The foundation is committed to expanding opportunity and ensuring a more equitable future for all in the Bay Area. Working with its donors, it distributed nearly

$100 million to nonprofit organizations last year. The San Francisco Foundation serves Alameda, Contra Costa, Marin, San Francisco and San Mateo counties.

Fred Blackwell

Who has had the greatest influence on you as a professional?

I tell this story often. The most influential people in my career have been family members. It comes from both sides of my family. Most of my career has been around social justice because of my mother, and around the importance of place because of my grandfather. On my mother's side, I come from a family of nonprofit professionals and community organizers. From a very early age, I was exposed to this part of the world of work. I was exposed to concepts of social and economic justice. I went to the school founded by the Black Panther Party in Oakland, California, I often say, as a result of spending all that time with my mother and uncle.

On my father's side is an unlikely influence. My grandfather grew up in South Carolina and moved to Harlem, where he was eventually able to open a bar and grill around the corner from the Apollo Theater. He said two things. One was: "When you leave New York, you are not going anywhere." The other was: "If it's not a Cadillac, it's not a car." At the time, driving a Cadillac in Harlem was the ultimate. I used to visit my grandparents and spend time at the bar. My grandfather's connection to that place influenced me.

Thus far, what have been the worst and best events in your life, and what did those experiences teach you?

I will start with the worst. This is my second tour of duty at the San Francisco Foundation. My first was as a fellow. I stayed on after my fellowship to work on a project with the Hewlett Foundation to take a comprehensive community revitalization project in West Oakland, where I grew up. I went in bright-eyed and bushy-tailed. At the time, there was a kind of apathetic leadership in City Hall around revitalization issues, and I got really mired in the neighborhood politics. I struggled around two foundations working with one another. I was also trying to play an operational role in a very low-income community. It didn't go well. There were a number of things I learned. One was that it is nearly impossible to organize a community around money, particularly one that is not a wealthy one. Money, as a tool to dangle in front of folks, was not the right tool. There were all kinds of issues about race and ethnicity that surfaced. I was really disappointed, but I draw on what I learned from that project frequently.

My proudest moment was when I was working for Gavin Newsom in San Francisco. The mayor hired me to take from soup to nuts the concept of making local government more responsive to schools and neighborhoods struggling the most. We found that half of the families where the kids were being removed from their homes lived within walking distance of one of the Seven Corners, which was the Skid Row of San Francisco. We designed a program to go to the residents and ask them how services could lead to better outcomes. I was knocking on doors throughout the community.

One particular place was the Alice Griffith housing project in Bayview-Hunters Point. The residents were the most upset and most ready to make a change. All the things we were talking about would not take hold because housing conditions were so deplorable. We had to combine that work by tearing down the housing without displacing the people.

We put together a program and a finance plan. After making promises we were not sure we could keep, we got a Choice Neighborhood Grant and made it happen. That was a pretty profound moment. We have been raising private dollars at the San Francisco Foundation. It is in the third of five phases of development, and people are living in it.

What, if anything, keeps you up at night?

We have embarked on a very ambitious agenda for the Foundation, which is putting race and class at the forefront, so that the rising tide lifts all boats. It's an issue that is so much larger and more complex than the Foundation can address on its own. The magnitude of that challenge and keeping it feasible are what keep me up at night.

What is your philosophy of life?

I have a quote in my office from Benjamin Elijah Mays [the civil rights leader and president of Morehouse College from 1940 to 1967]. He said the true tragedy is not *not* achieving your goals, it is not having goals for which you are reaching. Having goals, taking risks and not being afraid to fail are very important things to keep in mind, particularly working in the social change world. It's important to swing for the fence and have realistic, attainable goals that are still ambitious and bold. You can't be afraid not to reach those goals. My philosophy is about being bold, but not careless and frivolous, particularly in a country where we have set some very lofty goals that have not been reached yet.

What is the greatest misconception about you?

I come across as pretty laid-back, easy-going and friendly. But underneath that is a tremendous amount of intensity around what needs to be accomplished. The misconception is that the laid-back exterior means a lack of intensity.

What is the most important thing you tell young people who are thinking about making careers in the nonprofit sector?

I try not to let this come off the wrong way. I believe very strongly that there is a difference in the sector between social service and social change. People need to identify early on in this field which one they're engaged in. Social service to me is something that can be turned off and on. You can turn off the lights and go home. Social change is a lifestyle that calls on you to do things in ways that are a little bit different, edgier, and more fearless.

In some of my recent commencement speeches, I have talked about the difference between a rock and a coffee bean. If you put a rock in water, it will displace the water, but the water will return to its original state. If you put a coffee bean in water, it changes the taste and texture. When you remove the bean, it looks and tastes different. I always tell young people to seek to be a coffee bean.

What new opportunities do you see for your organization in the next five years?

We have pushed all our chips in the middle of the table around a bold equity agenda for greater racial and economic inclusion in the Bay Area region. That is at least a 10-year focus for the Foundation. I feel it is the defining challenge of our time. We have this fabulous economy here, with limitless opportunity, and there's almost a Gold Rush mentality, but many people feel locked out. There are many people in the Bay Area who have been working on this for years on the ground, but they've been operating without an adequate amount of support and cover from the public sector. We are actively engaged with our grantees and donors. With the partnership and support of our Bay Area Leads donors, we are leveraging our reputation and grant-making as we expand and become more visible in our civic leadership role. We're hoping to enlarge the circle and shine a light on what works and what doesn't. We want to use our influence to bring a new set of players to the table and hopefully tap into the passions and interests of Bay Area philanthropists so they'll want to join us in addressing equity in the Bay Area.

How are the choices of the very wealthy private philanthropists influencing traditional foundation giving?

That's a great question, and one we grapple with frequently. The way this gets characterized, at least in the Bay Area, is that on one hand you have the folks who have newfound wealth and are bringing a greater level of commitment to impact measurement and data. People describe a traditional approach to philanthropy that seeks a different kind of impact, and I feel that is a false dichotomy. People with newfound wealth could learn a lot from established philanthropic individuals and institutions so they don't repeat the mistakes of others. I think those engaged in more traditional philanthropy could also learn from the former group. We should be aiming for a sweet spot between the two groups.

What is the one thing you would say to your colleagues who are leading nonprofits seeking foundation funding?

We understand that we are a foundation in the business of providing grants and fueling the works of nonprofits. I would really like them to look at us as partners, and think not only of how we can provide funding for their work, but how we can use our reputation and influence to change the trajectory of how things are happening in their communities. I want to go beyond the transactional and move to more of the transformational. Part of it is us making ourselves available and articulating our desire to be in that kind of relationship.

CHAPTER 21

Persist

Our nonprofit sector leaders worked, often for years, to prove their concepts. Then they worked, again often for years, to expand the impact of their solutions. Many of them say they are surprised by how long it took. But they did not (and do not) give up. Here are some of their tips for succeeding over the long term.

A. You Cannot Win Every Battle

Evan Wolfson, of Freedom to Marry, says, "In the most important speech I've ever given, 'Marriage Equality and the Lessons for the Scary Work of Winning,' two of the lessons I put forward were Lesson 1: 'Win trumps loss.' You're always going to have losses, but if you achieve your wins, they will enable you to cover your losses. Lesson 2: Of course, you should aim to win, but when you can't, you should at least fight and engage, so that you lose forward. You can't win every time. You're going to lose. There are going to be losses. ... Be clear about where you're going and what you want to achieve."

B. Profound Change Takes Time

Most of our interviewees are working toward big goals. Some other examples include ending childhood hunger in the United States, halving deaths from gun violence by 2025, and ending poverty in New York City. It takes tenacious, patient leadership to be willing to tackle these kinds of problems. These issues did not develop overnight, and finding and implementing solutions will require determined effort.

Larry Kramer of the Hewlett Foundation, speaking of the latest trends in philanthropy, says, "Dealing with social problems like poverty, racism, climate change or income inequality is not like developing a new piece of software. Progress is slow not from lack of imagination or willingness to take chances, but because the problems are *hard*. Addressing them requires patience and perseverance, coupled with a willingness to learn continuously and a lot of humility."

James Siegal, CEO of KaBOOM! Inc., has a slightly different perspective. KaBOOM! is a nonprofit that provides opportunities for kids to play, particularly those living in poverty. It is famous for its work in the inner cities, where volunteers build a playground in six hours. But it is now moving beyond individual playgrounds to support the idea of "playability," or the extent to which an entire city is designed to support active play.

Siegal says, to both nonprofits and foundations, "Stop talking about the internal issues. Ask 'Are we having the right conversations with the people in power?' Is this the 'nice' sector or a critical partner? There is a difference between being effective and being transformative."

Some nonprofits are transformative. Some provide critical services. Both aim to improve life on this planet.

C. Achieve Life Balance

Several interviewees talk about the importance of balance to keep young people from burning out in the first 10 years of working in the sector. Bob Giannino, CEO of uAspire, which helps make college affordable for all qualified young people, says, "Sustainability in community work requires a good work-life balance. I cannot tell you how many 30-somethings have done this work for five to seven years and are already burnt out. They dive in, and that may not sustain over time. We need people who are committed to this work and can sustain themselves over this trajectory for decades."

Bill Ulfelder, New York State director of the Nature Conservancy, says, "If you wait to build your family time during spring breaks or sabbaticals, you've lost the opportunity to be deeply connected to your family. A lot of my dealings with Roger Milliken [my mentor] have been about how I want to show up as a husband to my wife and a father to my daughter. I realized that I need to prioritize work less and focus on my family, because that would ultimately allow me to be a better leader and more successful at work."

This may surprise someone who has never worked in the sector, but it does not surprise us. Nonprofits ask much of their employees. The urgency of the mission makes it hard to slow down. Whereas compensation in the private sector is likely to be commensurate with employees' hard work, people in the nonprofit sector are generally paid less. Nonprofit organizations attract more people with passion and commitment to a cause than those who are focused primarily on high salaries.

Counting on passion is not a sustainable solution to the problems that nonprofit sector organizations hope to solve. Dan Pallotta is known for his TED Talk on what is wrong with the nonprofit sector marketplace, which has over 4 million views as of this writing. He understands the necessity of increasing pay scales in the sector, among other things, to better attract and compensate talented people for their important work. Pallotta says our cultural mores and economic structure discriminate against the nonprofit sector: "If you want to make $50 million selling violent video games to kids, go for it, we will put you on the front cover of *Wired* magazine. But if you want to make half a million dollars curing kids of malaria, you are considered a parasite yourself."

CHAPTER 22

Robert H. Forrester

President and CEO, Newman's Own Foundation;
Executive Chairman, Newman's Own, Inc.

Bob Forrester became the first president of Newman's Own Foundation at the request of its founder, Paul Newman. After Newman died in 2008, Forrester assumed the additional role of chairman and CEO of the Newman's Own food company. In 2015, he became executive chairman of the company and continues as president and CEO of Newman's Own Foundation.

In 1980, he founded Payne, Forrester & Associates, LLC, a consulting group providing services to nongovernmental organizations in strategic planning, governance, communications and fund-raising. He was chairman and CEO until 2008.

From 1976 to 1980, he headed the New York University Development Office and was a member of the senior management team recruited to lead the turnaround of the then financially troubled university. From 1969-1975, he worked at the University of Hartford as director of development and special assistant to the president. Between 1979 and 1990, he built and owned Martha's Vineyard Cable Television Company and FM radio station, WMVY.

Forrester serves on several boards: CECP, University of Hartford, SeriousFun Children's Network, Safe Water Network, Newman's Own Foundation and Newman's Own, Inc. He also serves on advisory boards for Discovery Center, Connecticut Council of Philanthropy, the Centers for Truth, Racial Healing and Transformation of the American Association of Colleges and Universities, and Martha's Vineyard YMCA.

He holds a B.S. in psychology, served as an officer in the U.S. Army in Vietnam, and received honorary Doctor of Humane Letters degrees from Mount Holyoke College and the University of Hartford.

Newman's Own

Newman's Own combines two of the most widely admired aspects of the American character: business entrepreneurship and philanthropic generosity. Founded in 1982 by Paul Newman, the company began with a single product, an oil and vinegar salad dressing, and was guided by two principles; "Quality Will Always Trump the Bottom Line" and "All Profits to Charity." Paul started Newman's Own Foundation in 2005 to ensure that these founding principles would continue after his passing.

Today, Newman's Own, Inc., has over 300 food and beverage products, including salad dressings, pasta sauces, frozen pizza, salsa, refrigerated lemonades, cookies, snacks and pet food. Products are sold all over the world. Newman's Own Foundation continues Paul Newman's commitment to use all royalties and profits that it receives from the sale of its food products for charitable purposes. More than $500 million has gone to charity since 1982, supporting thousands of organizations worldwide. The primary focus areas include: encouraging philanthropy, children with life-limiting conditions, nutrition and empowerment.

Robert H. Forrester

Who has had the greatest influence on you as a professional?

As I've gotten older, I've found that the answer to that question depends on when you ask it. The more you go through life, the more it becomes a tapestry of people and events that influence one's life. If you had asked me that question when I was at New York University, I would have had one answer. Three years later, it might have been two or three different people. Then in my consulting business, I've met and worked with so many different people. Now, as president and CEO of Newman's Own Foundation, I would say the last person who really had a powerful influence on me, and was a good friend, was Paul Newman.

I can't think of a better way to be wrapping up a career and bringing together all my different values and ambitions than trying to help this extraordinary enterprise and continue Paul's legacy. Newman's Own is a true model of what it means to be engaged in the social, independent and philanthropic sector. Paul was an extraordinary guy. He had a sense of humility, and he never felt he was better or worse than the next person. His generosity was authentic and as unencumbered by philosophy as you can imagine. He epitomized things that I didn't even know were important to me in my life as I came to a certain age.

If you want to be specific, then I would say, "Let's talk about Paul Newman," but it would be awkward, because he never liked to be talked about, since he never thought what he was doing was special. Therefore, I'm a little hesitant to speak about him.

Thus far, what have been the worst and best events in your life, and what did those experiences teach you?

I think some of the worst things are also related to some of the best things. I could point to spending a year in Vietnam. Being in that situation as a young man awakened my understanding of the imbalance that exists in the world and my responsibilities in this world. The worst thing was sitting there in a combat area, and the best thing was that despite all that horror, I was learning and awakening. I was very lucky along the way to be able to work with mentors who were a lot older than me and were very significant people in their fields. I would say some of the most difficult moments were when these people I admired so much would take me to lunch and spend 30 minutes telling me what a good job I was doing, then they'd spend another 60 minutes telling me how I wasn't very good at certain things. It was frustrating, but when I look back, I'm surprised that individuals like these took time in their lives, for no reason I could understand, to spend with a young man and impart wisdom and lessons to him.

I could talk about how difficult it was to be the counsel to the American University of Beirut (AUB) when fighting was going on. AUB was a client for 12 years, and another person who had a great impact on my life, Malcolm H. Kerr, who was the president of the university, was assassinated. These were terrible things to experience, but at the same time, I can say the American University of Beirut was one of the most hopeful places I have ever been in. Despite such hostility, turmoil and danger, it stood as a beacon of hope.

Despite all the depressing, worrisome things you read about, it's been a privilege to travel the world and be in some of the worst areas, because I've seen average people trying to improve their own lives as well as the lives of the people around them—people they don't even know.

Has Newman's Own Foundation tried to scale its programs and operations?

Not really. What everybody at Newman's Own is trying to do is take our original fundamental values that were always part of Newman's Own, in terms of its business and philanthropy, and have a relevancy and impact in today's world. Paul never laid down the law about what we had to do. He figured that if he wasn't going to be a part of the future, then he had no reason or right to tell other people what to do.

When Paul founded Newman's Own Foundation in 2005, it was a great opportunity and privilege to work with him and get his guidance while he served as chairman, for almost four years. He was very active in every board meeting, so we were able to connect with his thinking. Out of this relationship, we fashioned four very broad areas that reflect a combination of factors that are enduring. Our No. 1 priority is to simply encourage philanthropic behavior. What that means is open to interpretation, but we deliberately use the word "philanthropy" because we feel it's really part of the human DNA, and the origin of the word is simply the love of humankind.

We've become much more organized in our thinking about being a risk-taker. We are not out to create a new way to solve the world's problems, and then have others come and ask for funding to implement our program. We always try to work with organizations that generate meaningful impact and improve the lives of others, which helps put a face on what we are doing and results in something bigger than just the services they provide.

For us, scaling is supporting our values and asking, "In this world, with our little resources, what can we do here?" Newman's Own has a respected credibility in terms of who we are, so when we do something, it may garner the attention of others who see what we can do. It's not about getting bigger, it's about getting smarter in terms of today's and tomorrow's world. Each generation requires a different kind of thinking. If you come to Newman's Own, you'll find an organization that is uncluttered with bureaucracy, committee meetings and processes. We are a very small company, which is one of the things we will keep. The intimacy of the organization is what gives us our specialness.

What are your priorities in your work and what proportion of your time do you spend on each of them?

The priorities will change and have changed in my work, because I see myself as an interim steward of this legacy, from a founder to its future. Right after Paul passed away, there were maybe two or three years of significant business challenges. Long-range strategy was something that was very hard to get to, because we had to go around the world and reassure people that Newman's Own was not going to change internally and externally. We were at a stage where things needed to be modernized, from a company that grew bit by bit over time into something that was competing with very big companies.

There was a period when many long-time employees retired, and we needed to hire senior management for Newman's Own, both in the food company and the foundation. So my time was spent trying to find people who not only had the leadership skills and competency to run a food company or a philanthropic foundation or intellectual property company, but who would also share the values and culture of Newman's Own. In our view, Newman's Own should not exist unless the feel of it endures.

Now I spend my time building the organization for the future, including succession for myself and at the board level. We have some legal issues related to structure that are very important to us, and I need to work out that part of the future of the organization. I do a great deal of work with our senior managers, trying to help them make good business decisions that reflect our values, because there are times when a business decision may be contrary to a value decision. One of Paul's values was that quality would always trump profits. You may be able to make a lot of money doing something, but if it isn't the right thing for us to do, we should step away. As the CEO, I can simply say no, but as the steward of a legacy, I really want to spend time with the senior managers, talking to them about why we make these decisions—because they are ultimately the ones who are going to be passing that on to the next generation.

I spend a great deal of time representing Newman's Own in the media and with our many stakeholders. It's complex because there is no other organization with a structure like Newman's Own, where the foundation owns an actual operating company. My role is constantly trying to orchestrate the pieces that have different operating imperatives into a kind of symphony. I also spend a lot of my time working directly with our strategic grantees, where my background can be most helpful. Inside the foundation, there is a group of our grantees with whom we have a long-term relationship.

For instance, SeriousFun Children's Network children's camps around the world are our most important strategic partnership. We have a big project in the water sector, Safe Water Network, and we have initiatives in the military veteran space and in the nutrition space. Those are strategic grantees as opposed to making smaller seed grants. SHOFCO (Shining Hope for Communities), an organization in Africa, started out with just a small girls' school, and it now reaches 180,000 individuals a year. As a strategic grantor, we provided significant funding, expertise and guidance, while avoiding telling them what to do.

What, if anything, is keeping you up at night?

Even though I'm not going to be a part of the future, it truly worries me. On a more personal level, I'm always asking myself if I've done everything I can for the legacy of Newman's Own, and if our people are feeling fully empowered. Is there more that I can do? Have I shared my experiences with enough younger people who might find some value in it?

I started a fellowship program inside Newman's Own. We are now in our second formal year of the program and have 17 fellows this year. Last year, we had 13 fellows. These are young people right out of college. I think one thing we're missing today is a connection between wisdom and wealth. Wealth now gets created so quickly and in such massive amounts, but it takes years of experience, frustration, failures and successes to create wisdom. I used to tell clients in my consulting practice that the best I could give them was my mistakes, so they could avoid them.

How important is it to find the right people for your board and what qualities do you seek? How successful have you been in matching those qualities?

I have a great board. My board has had to go through unique stages of growth. My view is that in a nonprofit organization, the ultimate charter lies with the board. The board is an institution of people. Management changes, but a board doesn't change if it's running properly. One of my areas of expertise in consulting is getting people to think about board management. Being a consultant and advising people is very different from being a CEO. We have two boards, and we are building them out to match the combination of competencies that we need on the boards and the values of who we are. I think we are doing a good job of that. On our food company board now, we have a leading professor of nutrition. That's a pretty bold thing for a food company, to have an academic person, and it's very important to me, because I want Newman's Own to always be trusted and seen as authentic.

I'm bringing on younger people because some of our board members are getting older. We need to refresh the board, and we're in the process of doing that now.

In the beginning, the people I put on the board had to know Paul Newman, so I had people like John Whitehead, former chairman of Goldman Sachs; Steve Reinemund, the former CEO of PepsiCo; and Josh Weston, former CEO of ADP, on the board. These were people of accomplishment and expertise and were known to be philanthropic. I knew they shared our core values.

At the end of the day, I want a board with competency and empathy that can distinguish its role from that of management, but still make management appropriately accountable. That's the absolute key to a mature, effective, always relevant nonprofit.

What is the most important thing you would tell a young person who is thinking about making a career in the nonprofit sector?

I would counsel them to make sure that they are, first and foremost, driven by a passion for the purpose of an organization, whether it's homelessness, nutrition, education or the environment, etc. Having that as your true north gets you through everything else. When you get into the sector and start working, it's real work. It's a job, and it's hard. You are going to have politics in any organization, management stresses, disappointments, conflicts and frustrations.

If you are working in the commercial sector, then they usually solve that problem with a big check, and that's your motivation. I always say, no matter where you are in a career, when you get to those tough moments, always try to get back in touch with the purpose of the organization. For instance, when we were dealing with building out these children's camps around the world, there were some really difficult times when cultures clashed. I would always pause conversations and say, "Let's just take a moment to think of what's in the best interest of the child."

I advise people to find an organization that is going to have a breadth of experience, because when they first start, they're not going to know all their opportunities or how they'll feel in any particular field. The broader your experience is, the easier it will be to identify where your path might take you. I mean broad in terms of the organization's mission as well as the functions and how they're handled. I would also advise them to understand the value of compound interest. I wish I had understood that.

We are in the midst of a national conversation about race and racial equity. What is your organization doing internally and externally to address racial inequity?

We don't just think about racial inequity. We have always thought broadly about inequity among all people and the fact that circumstances divide people when they shouldn't. Paul started a program called the Discovery Center, which we still fund. We have worked with children in a camp environment. Growing up, my family wasn't wealthy, and I went to a mixed school. If you're young enough, you don't understand the differences—whether it's disability or race, wearing glasses or not. All that stuff comes later, through different kinds of experiences. Part of our philosophy is if you can deal with this type of thing early enough, it doesn't have to be a profound, sustained experience.

A couple of years ago, Newman's Own underwrote the 50th Anniversary of the Civil Rights Act of 1964 exhibition at the Library of Congress, and I felt that we ought to take that moment and bring it out to our campuses, because I really believe that our campuses are significant places where civil dialogue should happen. I think they are meant to be places for learning and opening minds without condemning a whole class, and they've drifted in that regard.

We developed a program with the University of Hartford, called Empowering Change. It's doing very well at connecting all the different communities and institutions around a week's worth of experience and dialogue: students, faculty and community leaders. That model really showed us that campuses need to be a part of the dialogue.

We are partnering with the American Association of Colleges and Universities in a national program known as Centers for Truth, Racial Healing and Transformation, which is aimed at creating broad civil dialogue around race issues of all kinds in our country. American campuses must be part of this conversation. They are there to educate, open minds and be places for civil dialogue.

I think we need to engage at many different levels for a long time and probably forever, if we are going to keep enriching our society with a dialogue on the issues of difference, diversity and inequity. There is no doubt that this is a real racial issue, but it's also an issue of economics and opportunity.

A 2016 U.S. Trust study shows that high net worth Americans have greater confidence in individuals and nonprofits than in the executive branch or Congress. With the current administration and Congress, what role should the nonprofit sector and organizations like yours play over the next several years?

We have to be very careful not to get into the politics of everything. Once you are in that swamp, particularly with things as highly charged as they are now, you will always be identified in that swamp. The nonprofit sector can do a number of things, like create and promote programs that deal with the core issues that have led our country to where it is today. These are issues of imbalance and economic inequalities. I question some aspects of big entitlement programs, because they can diminish people's dignity rather than empower them. If the nonprofit sector begins to look as if it's associating with a political side, it loses the ability to be an honest broker of that trust. It also raises the nonprofit world's visibility as a target of harmful tax legislation. You have to be careful there. It's important to be an independent voice.

The nonprofit sector also needs to demonstrate its own commitment to sorting things out inside our society. In many ways, the voices in the sector have become a bit too self-serving, thinking about preserving this or that, or too defensive. Our nonprofit sector is the envy of the world. One of the things that is unique about American society is that we have this third sector that is a competitor to government. It does everything except a few things that the government does, and it does them more effectively and efficiently.

There are issues with the media. We used to have a media that was informative and brokered diverse opinions. We don't have that anymore. We also have social media, which is among the most powerful things out there right now. How do you get that so it's not radicalizing the edges? I raise this question because I think the nonprofit sector, in a political way, has a role to play there.

After the 2016 election, *The New York Times* reported, "the widening political divergence between cities and small-town America also reflects a growing alienation between the two groups, and a sense—perhaps accurate—that their fates are not connected." What role should the nonprofit sector play in helping the two groups find common ground?

I really don't know the facts about the urban and suburban areas, and that, to me, is a major worry point that is not being well addressed. In Connecticut, we have the wealthiest suburbs in America, as well as the poorest cities. Those cities are mostly made up of minorities. Hartford used to be one of the most affluent cities in America, and now it's one of the poorest. It's probably 90 percent minorities, and surrounded by enormously wealthy suburbs that are 90 percent white.

There's no county government, so there's no regional solution, and it's very worrisome to me. This is where private foundations need to play a much greater role, because they are some of the few institutions that can bridge the divide. It's interesting because in the Hartford area, we have a really liberal community in the suburbs, until you talk to them about sharing some of their tax dollars with the city. Then they become a "No, not my way, not in my backyard" type of organization. I think the volatility and stress line in our society today is around this urban/suburban issue more than any other kind of geographic issues we have. If you look at where the problems have been happening, like the ones reported in the media, they are the older cities that have this kind of issue. And it's necessary for foundations to take a look at that.

If there were one thing you could say to your colleagues at other grant-making foundations, what would it be?

I hate to preach to others, but I would tell all my colleagues who have the opportunity to be on the giving side to go out and spend a lot of time (almost intern) with the non-profits. You can't be a truly effective grant-maker unless you have real empathy for what these people do and how, when they go out to see a funder, they wear their best clothes. That, to us, is the most fun. We are as much inside, in terms of feeling the challenges they have and having them be straightforward with us.

CHAPTER 23

Amy Houston

Managing Director of Management
Assistance, Robin Hood Foundation

Amy Houston runs management assistance at Robin Hood. She is also an adjunct faculty member at Columbia University's MBA program, where she teaches a course on high performing nonprofits. She chairs the Finance Committee of the board of the Leo Baeck Institute in New York and the Audit Committee of the board of the Nichols School in Buffalo.

She serves on the MBA Advisory Board at Tuck School of Business in Hanover, New Hampshire.

Prior to Robin Hood, she was a vice president at Aspect Education, a private company running language schools worldwide. She joined Aspect's senior team just after its purchase from Sylvan Learning Systems in 2000; the company was sold successfully to Kaplan in 2006. She was a principal consultant with the higher education and nonprofit practice at PWC and the general manager of Reading in Motion, an education reform organization in Chicago. She co-founded and served on the board of the Mad Housers of Chicago, a homeless advocacy organization. Houston earned a bachelor's degree from Georgetown University and an M.B.A. from the Tuck School of Business at Dartmouth College.

Robin Hood

Robin Hood is New York's largest poverty-fighting organization, and since 1988 has focused on finding, funding, and creating programs and schools that generate meaningful and measurable results for families in New York's poorest neighborhoods. Since its founding, Robin Hood has raised more than $2.5 billion in dollars, goods and services to provide hundreds of the most effective soup kitchens, homeless shelters, schools, job-training programs and other vital services that give New York's neediest citizens the tools they need to build better lives. Robin Hood's board of directors pays all administrative, fund-raising and evaluation costs, so 100 percent of donations go directly to organizations helping New Yorkers in need.

The Robin Hood model combines targeted funding with management assistance (MA) to support its nonprofits in strengthening their performance. The MA team is comprised of experienced consultants who are skilled at adapting business strategies to the challenges facing nonprofit organizations. Robin Hood recruits New York City's top firms to offer pro bono and fee based services, as well as talented professionals to serve on grant recipient boards. Consulting and training areas include governance, strategy, human capital, marketing, fund-raising, finance, technology, legal and real estate.

Amy Houston

Who has had the greatest influence on you as a professional?

Karl Andros is one of the first executive directors I worked for. He is still a good friend and mentor. He started his career as a musician and began playing weekday gigs in public schools. He quickly learned the ways that the performing arts could engage students—and he ultimately discovered the potential of the arts to become a powerful means of teaching reading and writing.

Now his organization, Reading in Motion, has been doing this work for 30-plus years. Every year, the program aggressively changes and improves. He is most inspiring to me because he is never resting. He is constantly asking questions and constantly looking for new and better ways to work. And, most importantly, he inspires that in everyone around him.

Thus far, what have been the worst and best events in your life, and what did those experiences teach you?

The best thing in my life goes back to working for Reading in Motion in the mid-nineties. I was a young, non-profit executive, raising money and trying to figure out how to run a business. I had this extraordinary board of directors who were all mid-career professionals. They were passionate about our mission—and fascinated by the prospect of taking the best tools from their big corporations and making them work for our $2 million nonprofit. The CFO of Leo Burnett helped us develop an operating reserve to both improve cash flow management and mitigate risk. The human resources lead from First Chicago had us doing 360 reviews for each member of our staff. We did our first ever five-year plan with the head of strategy at Quaker Oats.

These tools—and the art of applying them in the non-profit space—felt incredibly important to me. I decided to go to business school and bring this thinking back to the nonprofit sector. That has been my journey.

Now at Robin Hood, I get to do this every day. We study the private sector, which devotes incredible resources to R&D. We take what they learn and apply it to help our community partners run smart and lean. Today, the biggest areas of opportunity are in technology. We recently launched an initiative that employs texting to send updates and reminders to parents in schools and participants in job training programs. Related, we are helping our partners think through new cyber security threats—and how to put cost effective protections in place.

What, if anything, keeps you up at night?

There are so many things to be concerned about right now. The best place for me to channel concerns is in making positive change where I can.

So, I think a lot about how to solve problems. The good news is that at Robin Hood and in the nonprofit sector at large, there are lots of meaty problems to solve. And frankly, there are far fewer solutions than people like to acknowledge—and very few great solutions. The trick is identifying them, and then scaling them if they can be scaled.

I think technology holds massive promise. One of my former students founded an organization called City Health Works. They train community members to be health coaches who make house calls and ensure the basics are in place: nutrition and medication and the like. They use technology to gather data on patient progress and support the coaches. It's very simple technology for a very people-centered program.

What is your definition of happiness, or, what is your philosophy of life?

Happiness is when you are in pursuit of a challenging and interesting question, and you get to work on it every day. I get to do that at a place that works on the problem I care about most: giving every kid the same opportunity, the same starting place. At the end of the day, the happiness comes from the challenging and stimulating questions. How do you get from A to B smartest, fastest, cheapest? How do you slice data to bring a new insight? How do you solve a tricky issue between two team members? I try to balance that with all the other things I enjoy like taking a long hike, playing spades with my teenagers and husband or a few uninterrupted hours with a good book.

What is the greatest misconception about you?

A misconception about me personally and about the work we do at Robin Hood is that we value data more than the human aspect of our work. The misconception is that you must choose between head and heart. This is a false dichotomy. I believe the two things inform, push and balance one another. They can exist in the same space.

What is the most important thing you tell young people who are thinking about making careers in the nonprofit sector?

It is much harder to find resources than it is to find ideas. Fund-raising is not for the faint of heart. Smart people understand how challenging it is to build sustainable revenue models in our space—and every new social change organization must tackle this question head on.

Related, everyone who wants to do this work has to sell. Everyone needs to talk compellingly about the work and why it matters. Marketing, messaging and public speaking are all critical. As a result, everyone must get really good at this.

For people thinking about career development, go deep on one thing and gain a real skill set. Work for someone who is really talented and really energizing. The nonprofit sector still has so much to learn from what the best private sector organizations are doing in terms of talent development. If you can find a nonprofit that lives and breathes a commitment here, sign on fast.

What new opportunities do you see for your organization in the next five years?

We have been in this business for almost 30 years. The model has always been to take this year's funding and invest it the next year. But complex problems take longer.

Testing and perfecting takes more than a year. The question is how do we keep the direct and urgent nature of the current model and balance it against moving the needle on longer-term issues?

This is also an interesting time for collaboration. The problem in the sector is we have all these different people with great ideas. Robin Hood is really a collection of a couple thousand of these people who say that fighting poverty is the goal and we are going to invest in that together. But how do we do that in an even more significant way with donors? For so long, we have done the thinking, and our donors have provided the capital. But now we are doing a lot more co-creating. We are increasingly the place where folks come to see their big ideas brought to life, made stronger by our experience and the skills of the team. So the big question: How do we deepen and magnify the best ideas out there?

We are in the midst of a national conversation about race and racial equity. What is your organization doing, both internally and externally, to address racial inequity?

This is the heart of our mission, yet there is so much more we must do to be better. Every conversation about poverty is also a conversation about race. The injustice woven into the fabric of our society is finally gaining traction in our national conversation, but we have so far to go. Externally Robin Hood is focused on elevating the perspectives and experiences of people living in poverty. They should not be the subjects of the conversation. They should be driving the conversation.

Internally, we are thinking about diversity, inclusion, representation and equity—evolving the culture of Robin Hood together. We are at our best when every member of the team feels understood, heard, valued and engaged. How do we work in a more thoughtful, responsive and proactive way together? Like most things at Robin Hood, smart and passionate team members will come up with ideas and my job is to find ways to spread them across the organization.

How are the choices of very wealthy private philanthropists influencing traditional foundation giving?

Robin Hood's donors focus laser-like on those who have less. It's that clarity of mission—and collection of talents and energy—that gives Robin Hood its power. Every donor knows they can do more collectively than alone. Because of this, Robin Hood is one of the best continuing experiments in collaborative social change.

What is the one thing you would say to your colleagues who are leading nonprofits seeking foundation funding?

People with clear vision win the game. Have confidence in and clarity about the product you are delivering. Robin Hood and our funding peers are far more pliable than folks realize and far more flexible in working to support great models. We are at our best when we are listening, learning and then hustling in response.

Do one thing incredibly well versus trying to do a little bit of everything. The biggest mistake people make is being too focused on problems and less focused on effective solutions. We have direct conversations with organizations seeking funding—and the biggest reason we turn groups down is because the program doesn't do enough. The program may make life better for someone in poverty—but it is not responsible for changing a life trajectory. With so much at stake, it is imperative that we focus on the programs that actually change a life.

CHAPTER 24

Larry Kramer

President, William and Flora Hewlett Foundation

Larry Kramer has been president of the William and Flora Hewlett Foundation since 2012. Under his leadership, the foundation has maintained its commitment to areas of enduring concern, while adapting its approaches and strategies to meet changing circumstances and seize new opportunities. He has been instrumental in launching new efforts to respond to pressing and timely problems, such as challenges related to political polarization and cybersecurity.

Before joining the foundation, Kramer served from 2004 to 2012 as Richard E. Lang Professor of Law and dean of the Stanford Law School. During his tenure, he spearheaded significant educational reforms, pioneering a new model of multidisciplinary legal studies while enlarging the clinical education program and incorporating a public service ethos.

At the start of his career, he served as law clerk to U.S. Court of Appeals Judge Henry J. Friendly of the Second Circuit Court and U.S. Supreme Court Justice William J. Brennan, Jr. Following his clerkships, Kramer served as professor of law at the University of Chicago and University of Michigan law schools. He joined the faculty of New York University School of Law in 1994, where he served as associate dean for research and academics and Russell D. Niles Professor of Law, before leaving for Stanford University in 2004.

Kramer is a fellow of the American Academy of Arts and Sciences and a member of the American Philosophical Society and the American Law Institute. He serves as a director on the boards of a number of nonprofit organizations, including the National Constitution Center, Independent Sector and the ClimateWorks Foundation.

He received an A.B. in psychology and religious studies from Brown University in 1980, and a J.D. from the University of Chicago Law School in 1984.

William and Flora Hewlett Foundation

The William and Flora Hewlett Foundation is a nonpartisan, private charitable foundation that advances ideas and supports institutions to promote a better world.

For more than 50 years, the foundation has supported efforts to advance education for all, preserve the environment, improve lives and livelihoods in developing countries, promote the health and economic well-being of women, support vibrant performing arts, strengthen San Francisco Bay Area communities and make the philanthropy sector more effective.

The foundation was established in 1966 by engineer and entrepreneur William R. Hewlett and his wife, Flora Lamson Hewlett, with their eldest son, Walter Hewlett. Today, it is one of the largest philanthropic institutions in the United States, awarding roughly $400 million in grants in 2016 to organizations across the globe to help people build better lives. Its philanthropic approach, and core areas of grant-making, remain connected to the ethos and values of its founders.

Established through the personal generosity of the Hewlett family, the foundation is wholly independent of the Hewlett Packard Company and the Hewlett Packard Company Foundation.

Larry Kramer

Who has had the greatest influence on you as a professional?

A couple of people, actually. John Sexton was dean when I was at New York University Law School. From him I learned generosity. There are leaders for whom the goal is to get from you as much as they can while giving as little as they have to, but a good leader gives as much as he can while asking for no more than he needs.

Geoffrey Stone, who was dean when I taught at the University of Chicago Law School, showed me what it means to have integrity in a leadership position. That's more challenging than you might think. Geoff was a role model for being honest and forthright and staying true to his and his institution's values.

Paul Brest was my predecessor at both Stanford and Hewlett. I don't know a better way to put this than to say that he showed me how to run an institution with class. Paul embodies all the best qualities of good leadership, and he makes it seem effortless—which it isn't.

I clerked for Justice William Brennan, Jr., and from him I learned the importance of being transparent. Where the other justices played their cards close to the chest, Justice Brennan encouraged us to share our thinking fully, freely and openly. In the end, we got more back than we would have otherwise. That is a lesson I have tried to follow in all my jobs. Leading should be like playing five-card poker, but with all the cards up.

Thus far, what have been the worst and best events in your life, and what did those experiences teach you?

The worst thing that ever happened was my father's death. He wasn't a big talker, so I didn't understand how important he was to me until he died. He was a steady presence in the background, and the whole world felt different when he was no longer there. It was like losing a part of the background, whose importance in making you feel safe and at home wasn't apparent until it was gone.

The best thing was the birth of my daughter. The two events are related. After my dad died, I realized how relationships make your life. I could never replace the relationship I had with my father. There is nothing like it. And I wanted to experience that from the other side: as a parent to a child. It turned out to be every bit as overwhelming and wonderful as I had imagined, though totally different too.

This sense of the importance of relationships is something I take into my work. I spend a lot of time trying to create a sense of community at Hewlett. I really dislike the phrase "work-life balance." There is just life, and work is part of it. I want the people at Hewlett to have three-dimensional relationships with me and with each other, to feel that they are part of something that is more than just a job. When we disagree about work, there should be more than just work in our relationships to fall back on.

What, if anything, is keeping you up at night?

The Hewlett Foundation supports grantees tackling huge, complex challenges: combating climate change, alleviating global poverty, improving education in America. But solutions to all these problems require a functioning government. Observing what's happening today, I fear we may be witnessing the beginning of the end of American democracy. I know that sounds dramatic, but it just might be true. So that's what keeps me up at night.

Democracy is more than just voting. It's voting in a system in which everyone's participation is valued. And it is governing in ways that respect the legitimacy of opponents; that recognize the need for compromise; that let science and evidence shape policy; and that cherish a free press, an independent judiciary, and other critical political and civil institutions. Democracy presupposes ideological conflict, but it's supposed to be like *Fight Club*, governed by a political version of Marquess of Queensberry rules to keep it from becoming "Win at all costs."

Our leadership has forgotten that there are more important things than winning a policy fight today. The greatness of America has been as the most successful experiment in popular government of all time. That is so much more important than seesawing disagreements about free markets versus a mixed economy. The shortsighted people in power today, and I mean on both sides, have their priorities backwards and are grinding down the foundations on which our system rests. Worse, they are doing so with the support (or, possibly worse, the indifference) of large segments of the American people.

I don't know if philanthropy can help fix this. People in democratic societies, it is said, get the government they deserve. But there may be things we can do to preserve or reawaken awareness of the attitudes and institutions and practices that are needed to make democracy work. We think we have to try, in any event, which is why we launched the Madison Initiative in 2013.

What is your definition of happiness, or, what is your philosophy of life?

I try to make relationships matter. I don't want to fall out with people over abstractions like politics or religion, not when I have concrete day-to-day experiences with them that should matter more. I also think you have to live your life with integrity, which means being honest with yourself about motives and goals and attending to the consequences of your actions. I try very hard to live in such a way that I can take chances and try new things but won't have to regret what I have done.

I think it's important to admit when you're wrong. People tell me I'm stubborn, because I like to argue and will stick to my position for as long as I think I am right. And there's something to that. But I'm also pragmatic, and I actually like to change my mind. It's more important to get something right going forward than it is to win an argument. I get worried if too much time passes without my having changed my mind about something.

What is the most important thing you tell young people who are thinking about making careers in the nonprofit sector?

I tell them to follow their noses. The biggest mistake young people make, in my view, is choosing to do things that others tell them they should do if they want to get ahead, or choosing to do things because they think it's what others expect them to do. I tell young people to do something they feel passionate about. Then see where that leads and what opportunities it creates. That's been my own approach to life. I never had a long-term plan. Each step was an unanticipated consequence of something earlier. But I wouldn't have done it any other way. I think long-term life plans lead people into doing things they don't enjoy.

How are the choices of the very wealthy private philanthropists influencing traditional foundation giving?

Two things that are not always appreciated have shaped the new generation of wealthy philanthropists. First, many of them became wealthy early in life, and they are mostly still young (as these things go). Second, they are objects of media fascination, celebrities whose philanthropic choices are scrutinized very publicly. The Hewletts acquired their wealth gradually, without media scrutiny, and this enabled them to learn over time what mattered to them and how to do philanthropy well. Today's mega-rich don't have that luxury. The results are not always good, particularly when combined with the confidence, often bordering on arrogance, that great success at an early age brings.

This has led some of them to look down on and denigrate the veterans in the field. Traditional philanthropy has "failed," they say, and confidently predict that they can do better by being more "innovative" and "entrepreneurial," and by using new tools and "disruptive" thinking.

This could be good, and, at worst, it may be harmless. It could be good because they may well find new ways to do things from which we can all learn. That would be great. But this could also turn out to be just so much Silicon Valley prattle. The truth is, they are still learning, and who knows where they will end up? The good ones, I suspect, will discover that folks like John D. Rockefeller, Andrew Carnegie, and, yes, Bill Hewlett and Dave Packard, have more to teach them than they realize.

The notion that traditional philanthropy has "failed" strikes me as particularly naïve. By what measure? Dealing with social problems like poverty, racism, climate change or income inequality is not like developing a new piece of software. Progress is slow not from lack of imagination or willingness to take chances, but because the problems are *hard*. Addressing them requires patience and perseverance, coupled with a willingness to learn continuously and a lot of humility.

Yet the new philanthropists are definitely influencing traditional foundations—and not necessarily for the better. The attention and praise lavished on them has created a kind of insecurity in the field, a fear of seeming stodgy and behind the times. There's a sudden rush to change how we work, to try out the latest shiny objects. Worse, there has been a pronounced shift toward big, splashy efforts, coupled with demands for quick results. With all the hype, I worry that too many funders are moving away from what we and they do best.

If there were one thing you could say to your colleagues who are leading grant-seeking organizations, what would it be?

Be honest with us. Recognize that we cannot accomplish our goals without you, and that we need you as much as you need us. If it seems there's a power imbalance between funder and grant-seeker, recognize that if you aren't honest, and don't tell us what you really need, we can't provide it. We're not thin-skinned prima donnas. Really. So don't just tell us what you need—tell us, also, if we're making your work more difficult. I cannot promise we will always agree or do what you want, but let us at least have a relationship built on candor. The NGOs that work that way are our best partners. And I believe we are theirs.

CHAPTER 25

Leverage Your Success

If you have been fortunate, as well as diligent, and achieved at least some of your social change goals, you are ready to leverage your success. How will you know you have reached your goal? In some instances, as with same-sex marriage, it is easy to measure success. Either same-sex marriage is legal in your community, or it is not.

With other goals, like ending childhood hunger in the United States, measuring success is more difficult. Share our Strength, with its No Kid Hungry campaign, has adopted a few key measurements—such as kids getting healthy breakfasts at school, and having access to healthy food during the summer—to evaluate whether or not it has achieved its goal. Share our Strength has been tracking these measurements, and its CEO, Bill Shore, is confident that childhood hunger in the United States can be ended in five to eight years. Now that is reason to celebrate!

Many organizations will never completely achieve their goals. There will always be more children to educate and more people to heal. Here are a few principles for creating long-term sustainability for your organization.

A. Train Others

Evan Wolfson of Freedom to Marry is unusual in that he has dismantled his organization, since it accomplished its goal of making gay marriage legal in most of the United States. Wolfson now spends much of his time training groups in other countries on how to work toward legal gay marriage. He also advises U.S. groups, such as the National Immigration Law Center, which defends and advances the rights of low-income immigrants.

Of the organizations we encountered during this process, Freedom to Marry is the only one to have disbanded. Many will be around for a long time.

American Express has a long-term commitment to training the next generation of nonprofit leaders. Tim McClimon, president of the American Express Foundation, says, "We're committed to doing [leadership development] over the long haul. We don't see that as a temporary kind of thing. It's an almost forever thing, although one cannot commit to doing it forever. But, as a business, we do have a long-term commitment to leadership development." In 10 years, American Express has trained over 25,000 nonprofit leaders worldwide. We salute it for this achievement.

B. Work Toward Organizational Sustainability

In our experience, achieving organizational sustainability is one of a nonprofit's greatest challenges. We are often called in to consult precisely because an organization needs help learning how to sustain itself.

We are not talking about foundations, which have endowments to support them. We are talking about organizations primarily supported by philanthropy, such as uAspire, the Nature Conservancy, PBS and the Ms. Foundation for Women. In other words, this is a concern of at least half the leaders we interviewed.

Jim Gibbons is president and CEO of Goodwill Industries International, sometimes described as the first social enterprise. Goodwill raises philanthropic dollars. It also has a vast network of stores across the country generating revenue through sales. Gibbons says, "I think society has an expectation of a nonprofit behaving like a charity, as opposed to an efficient asset for the community. That can happen, especially in the social enterprise model, as the organization strives to find the sweet spot between impact and income. That is a challenge for the next 10 to 15 years. People have to learn to articulate and differentiate between fund-raising and revenue generation."

We bring up Goodwill because we believe organizations must seriously consider opportunities to create earned revenue. It is much easier for some types of organizations to generate income than it is for others. Museums can have members and create stores. Social service organizations must be more creative. Developing new sources of earned income is difficult and risky, but it is worth the effort of exploring whether it can be a possibility.

C. Plan for the Inevitable

We hear a lot about succession planning at conferences and leadership trainings. Our experience is that many non-profit organizations devote little or no time to this important management task. Smaller organizations in particular need to think strategically about succession, yet they have fewer resources to devote to it. In our interviews, we decided to approach this issue by asking leaders what advice they would give to a person stepping into their shoes if they were unable to perform their duties tomorrow.

Paula Kerger of PBS says that if tragedy were to strike, leaders should ensure that the organization moves forward without a hitch. "I am a firm believer in the importance of ... having leaders in place who are prepared to take the helm. At PBS, we spend a lot of time on succession planning for key positions across the organization." It is best to have designated a No. 2, even if one knows that person will not be the person picked to be the next CEO.

Darlene Fedun, CEO of Bethel Woods Center for the Arts, a cultural institution at the site of the 1969 Woodstock Festival, has this advice. "Leave your ego at the door, hire good people, provide a productive environment for them, coach and counsel them well, and you will succeed."

Marcy Syms, philanthropist and president of the Sy Syms Foundation, has an unusual approach to succession planning. She is "looking at spending down all the assets of the foundation and closing it down in my lifetime to make a bigger impact." She is concerned about many issues, including overpopulation and freedom of speech, and she wants to see more progress.

CHAPTER 26

Leon Botstein
President, Bard College

Leon Botstein, conductor, music historian and leader in education reform, has been president and Leon Levy Professor in the Arts and Humanities of Bard College since 1975. The author of *Jefferson's Children: Education and the Promise of American Culture*, he has published widely in the fields of music, education, and history and culture. Founder of Bard High School Early College, he has been a pioneer in linking American higher education to public secondary schools.

He has also overseen the establishment of Bard undergraduate and dual degree programs worldwide, with campuses in Russia, Germany, East Jerusalem and Kyrgyzstan, among others. Botstein is also a renowned international conductor who has served as the music director and conductor of the American Symphony Orchestra since 1992, artistic co-director of SummerScape and of the Bard Music Festival, and music director of The Orchestra Now (TŌN), as well as conductor laureate of the Jerusalem Symphony Orchestra, and artistic director of the Grafenegg Campus and Academy. His honors include the Award for Distinguished Service to the Arts from the American Academy of Arts and Letters, and Harvard University's Centennial Award, as well as the Cross of Honor from the Republic of Austria.

Bard College

Bard College is a four-year residential college of the liberal arts and sciences, with a 155-year history of academic excellence. Bard's campus consists of nearly 1,000 parklike acres in the Hudson River Valley. The college offers bachelor of arts degrees with nearly 50 academic programs in four divisions—arts; languages and literature; science, mathematics and computing; social studies and interdivisional programs and concentrations. Bard also bestows several dual degrees, including a B.A./B.S. in economics and finance, and at the Bard College Conservatory of Music, where students earn a bachelor's degree in music and a B.A. in another field in the liberal arts or sciences. Bard's distinguished faculty includes winners of MacArthur Fellowships, National Science

Foundation grants, Guggenheim Fellowships, Grammy Awards, French Legion of Honor awards and Pulitzer Prizes.

In addition to undergraduate academics, Bard operates 12 graduate programs and has expanded to encompass a network of regional, national and global partnerships—including dual-degree programs in four international locations; the Bard Prison Initiative, which grants college degrees to New York State inmates; and Bard High School Early Colleges, where students earn a high school diploma and an A.A. degree in four years. Bard's philosophy sets a standard for both scholarly achievement and engagement in civic and global affairs on campus, while also taking the College's mission to the wider world. The undergraduate college in Annandale-on-Hudson, New York, has an enrollment of more than 1,900 and a student-to-faculty ratio of 10:1.

Leon Botstein

Who has had the greatest influence on you as a professional?

My models are a mixture of influence. I have a strong admiration for the institution builders in the history of American higher education, including William Rainey Harper, the founding president of the modern University of Chicago, and James Bryant Conant, the president of Harvard, who had a very decisive influence in trying to direct the future of American public education in the postwar period. I'd also add activist and university/college president, Robert Maynard Hutchins, from the University of Chicago, and Theodore Hesburgh, the president of Notre Dame, who was a Jesuit priest and outspoken public figure. John Kemeny, the president of Dartmouth, who was a great mathematician, and David Riesman, the sociologist from Harvard, have influenced me. People who have influenced me intellectually include Hannah Arendt. She was one of my teachers as an undergraduate student, and she taught me the necessity of political engagement as an essential part of realizing one's freedom as a human being and one's responsibility to society.

Thus far, what have been the worst and best events in your life, and what did those experiences teach you?

By far the worst thing that ever happened to me was that I had a daughter who was killed at the age of 8. That puts all other disappointments and failures in relief. What I learned from it is that one needs to find a way to rescue victory from the jaws of defeat. Rather than turning disappointment and tragedy into an excuse for feeling like a powerless victim, I try to recognize the unintended gift that comes from tragedy and failure. It's like a prizefight: The key is having the ability to get up again after getting knocked down. The other important thing I learned is that you have to be fully aware of the tenuousness of any plan or any notion that you can control events. You can't control what happens, and you're constantly at the mercy of the unexpected.

Bad things allow you to always balance the relative values that you cherish and to cease being dependent on what other people think of you. You have to learn to be confident in the judgment that you make of what you think is right, as opposed to the popular perception. The right things may not always be the popular things.

What advice would you give to your peers in the nonprofit sector about building an institution?

The first and most important thing you have to have is an idea that you believe in. You need a purpose. We're not a business where the measurement of success is profit or wealth. In business, the ultimate arbiter seems to be net worth, the balance sheet, profit and loss, and shareholder value. Success is quantifiable, and if you're successful at selling a bad product and the public buys the bad product, you're still a success. In the world of nonprofit, quality is more important than money, and we are closer to churches than we are to businesses. A great church is not one that's rich. A great church mobilizes the community on behalf of virtue and provides comfort, courage and a sense of hope to its parishioners.

So whenever I'm motivated by an idea of what needs to be done and have a sense of how that idea can be delivered, the next step is to ask how it can be enlarged without diminishing its quality. The greatest physician in the world is not necessarily the person who reaches the largest number of people. It's the one with the most effective medical intervention that can be replicated; so that if you discover a cure for polio or another major disease, it can be distributed in a way that reaches a mass population.

In our case, we have several things we've done that we are seeking to broaden because they're replicable. They include improving secondary education in the United States. Starting in 2018, we'll have eight high school early colleges around the country in five cities. Providing a liberal arts college education to incarcerated people is something that we've been able to scale nationally. Then there's the extension of a liberal arts education to first-year university students outside the United States. We've been able to expand that to Europe and Asia. We also hope to broaden and secure the role of the performing and visual arts inside the university.

The idea is the crucial thing, and some things are not scalable. Intimacy is not scalable, despite Facebook. Friendship is not scalable, despite Facebook. Great teaching is probably, despite technology, not scalable in the technological sense, but it is scalable in the institutional sense. So one has to be careful not to measure the impact one has simply by the numbers or the reach. Saving a single life has merit that can't be undermined by its uniqueness. The smallest thing is a key to larger success. If it's not right in a micro sense, it won't be right in a macro sense.

What are your priorities at the college and what do you spend the majority of your time on?

The most important thing is to deliver, more than rhetorically, on the promise of the liberal arts, which are falsely pilloried in the press as impractical. Universities have failed to deliver on them in intelligent ways, and we have to find a much better way than what we do now. Bard has been a leader in trying to deliver the substance and the methods of teaching young people the excitement of learning, critical thought, skeptical inquiry and research, which are the skills that the liberal arts prize.

What, if anything, keeps you up at night?

In our society, there's an over-emphasis on wealth accumulation as the sign of excellence. So at Bard, we spend our time providing the excellence, and not the wealth accumulation. What worries me most is sustaining traditions of philanthropy. The new wealth is a little bit overwhelmed by its belief that people who get rich are smarter than everyone else. There was a time, at the turn of the century, when patrons like the Carnegies and the Rockefellers turned to religious leaders, scientists and educators to learn how to deliver greatness through their philanthropy.

Now there's a tendency for the rich to think they know better about things they know nothing about. So when you look at someone like myself and say, "If you're so smart, why aren't you rich?" this is a noxious form of arrogance. It's the same arrogance that says if it doesn't make money, it can't be good. The Ninth Symphony of Beethoven never made money. *Swan Lake* and *The Nutcracker* don't make money. So money and mass fame can't be the only yardstick of value.

What is your definition of happiness, or, what is your philosophy of life?

I don't have a philosophy of life. I do believe that the criterion for well-being is a belief in the reciprocal character of happiness. I'm only happy when I've done my part in bettering the well-being and happiness of others. I have the right to pursue my own happiness, but that happiness has to be defined reciprocally, meaning I can't be happy when others are not. I cannot live passively in a world where there is injustice, inequality, cruelty and poverty without actually assisting my fellow human beings.

What is the greatest misconception about you?

I would say the biggest misconception about me is that I'm gifted and arrogant, which I'm not. I'm just hard-working. Another would be that I do many things. I'm actually a creature of unbelievable consistency and habit. I've done all the same things all my life, and they're very limited. I do fewer things than most people do. I have no hobbies. I play no sports. I'm a fanatical worker, so I put all my eggs in very few baskets.

How important is it to find the right people for your board, and what qualities do you seek? How successful have you been at matching those qualities?

The board is a very specific instrument. When running an organization, you need the ability to recruit and motivate people who are better than yourself. The trick to building an organization is people, and they must be people of ambition and quality. You have to give them authority and visibility. Do not micromanage. We've been successful in this institution by recruiting first-rate people and giving them latitude, freedom, independence, autonomy and room to maneuver. When it comes to the board, its members are crucial instruments for raising money. Therefore, you have to have people on the board who enjoy raising money and are good at it.

A good board has to be one that takes responsibility for the bottom line by doing more than insisting on efficiency, financial probity and responsible financial management. It also has to take responsibility in providing the necessary supplement to earned income. A key part of that income is philanthropy, and the board has to take primary responsibility for that philanthropy.

What is the most important thing you tell young people who are thinking about making careers in the nonprofit sector?

They should stop thinking about careers and think about what they want to do with their lives. Nobody should go into the nonprofit sector unless motivated by some level of idealism or the chance to change reality. Dreaming is an important part of having a career in this area, because you have to believe in something and believe things should be different than the way you found them. In my 20s, I was given an opportunity that was considered unrealistic by everybody. I became president of a college, and the state of New York put out a warning that the college would close within a year of my appointment. That was Bard, and I'm still here 42 years later. When I took the job, no one thought the job I was given had any realistic chance of success.

The trick you need in this line of work is to believe that you can alter what other smart people consider to be unrealistic. The other trick in any career is not to follow an imitative path, and to see opportunity in business where other people don't. The trick is always to think in a somewhat contrarian manner. Don't follow the crowd. Go against the grain and pull the crowd toward you.

What opportunities do you see for Bard in the next five years?

I think the opportunities for Bard are defined by the change of political realities in the United States. The catastrophic turn of events in the presidential election presents an opportunity for Bard to make its case and disrupt business as usual. We need to find opportunities to set the bar higher for the quality of education, the importance of the arts, the significance of the pursuit of science and scholarship research, and the freedom of the individual. We need to improve opportunities for civil liberties and tolerance by being in the opposition and by being a point of resistance against the spread of hate, xenophobia and falsehood.

We're in the midst of a national conversation about race and racial inequity. What is Bard doing, both internally and externally, to address racial inequity?

Bard has about 5,700 degree candidates under its jurisdiction. Over half of them are people of color. In the elite colleges, it has the third-highest minority enrollment on its main campus. Over 20 percent of the student body is eligible for Pell Grants, so a major priority of the institution is to be a provider of high-quality education to the underserved and discriminated against.

I think diversity of the board is a symbolic matter. I don't think it should be an imposed requirement. Since inequality is correlated with race, there is nothing wrong with having a generous board of white folks putting money into helping those who are not white. I think it's important to have minority voices and people of color on the board, but it is not insurance. It's important to hear different points of view, but the diversity of points of view on a board doesn't necessarily correlate with race. A large portion of the African-American community in the United States is conservative socially, politically and financially, so the color of one's skin is not an assurance of intellectual diversity. I think the only diversity that cuts across race and class is gender. Gender diversity seems to me an absolute must-have.

With a new administration in Congress, what role should the nonprofit sector and organizations like Bard play over the next two to four years?

Leaders of nonprofit institutions need to be in the public eye, standing up for things they believe in rather than hiding behind their jobs and keeping their noses to the grindstone. They should use their public positions as voices for what they believe to be right.

After the 2016 election, *The New York Times* reported, "the widening political divergence between cities and small-town America also reflects a growing alienation between the two groups, and a sense—perhaps accurate—that their fates are not connected." What role should the nonprofit sector play in helping the two groups find common ground?

Those of us in universities have an obligation to find a way to speak to people who fear and disagree with us or see us as out-of-touch elites. At Bard, we don't possess arrogance or smug liberalism if we're talking about opposition to the policies of the Trump administration or the Republican Party. To open a conversation with people who don't trust us, we have to be able to speak plainly, directly and persuasively. They don't believe we're patriotic or that we're concerned with the abandoned cities of the former industrial America. It's one of the faults of the Democratic Party. They abandoned this constituency and lost their capacity to talk to them, especially with the decline of unions and industrial America. There was a failure to communicate with people who disagree and have different traditions.

One of the things we try to do at Bard is improve the conversation by providing services, opening lines of communication, and working collaboratively with constituencies and communities with which we may actually disagree. For a long time, to our peril, we ignored communities of faith, believing somehow that religion was a dying phenomenon. We have to communicate with people who legitimately find comfort in faith and in communities of faith.

If there were one thing you could say to your colleagues leading grant-making foundations, what would it be?

Make large grants, take large bets, and don't spread the money so thinly that it makes no difference to the organizations. Stop this pattern of starting things but not sustaining them. Be more committed to sustaining the institutions in civil society that protect the fundamental values of the country. Be less interested in projects and more interested in institutional longevity and well-being.

CHAPTER 27

Evan Wolfson

Founder and President, Freedom to Marry

Evan Wolfson was founder and president of Freedom to Marry, the campaign that won marriage equality for homosexual couples in the United States, and is widely considered the architect of the movement that led to nationwide victory in 2015. In 1983, Wolfson wrote his Harvard Law School thesis on gay people and the freedom to marry. During the 1990s, he served as co-counsel in the historic Hawaii marriage case that launched the ongoing global movement for the freedom to marry, and has participated in numerous gay rights and HIV/AIDS cases.

Wolfson earned a B.A. in history from Yale College in 1978; served as a Peace Corps volunteer in a village in Togo, West Africa; and wrote the book *Why Marriage Matters: America, Equality, and Gay People's Right to Marry* (Simon & Schuster, 2004). Citing his national leadership on marriage and his appearance before the U.S. Supreme Court in *Boy Scouts of America v. James Dale, The National Law Journal* in 2000 named him one of "the 100 most influential lawyers in America." *Newsweek/The Daily Beast* dubbed him "the godfather of gay marriage" and *Time* magazine named him one of "the 100 most influential people in the world." In 2012, he received the Barnard Medal of Distinction alongside President Barack Obama.

Wolfson now devotes his time to advising and assisting diverse movements and causes in the United States and around the world. Based in New York City, he has been named a Distinguished Visitor from Practice at Georgetown Law Center, where he teaches law and social change, and senior counsel at Denton's, the world's largest law firm, with more than 125 offices in 50 countries.

Evan Wolfson

Who has had the greatest influence on you as a professional?

It's hard to pick just one. The person who first came to mind is Tim Sweeney. He's a close friend and one of the key people who brought me into the movement. He was my partner in developing Freedom to Marry and helped me in many of the phases—as a thought partner, a board member, a coach and also a funder, but really always essentially as a friend.

During our work together, Tim was for a period the head of the Gill Foundation, and prior to that, he was the program officer at the Evelyn & Walter Haas, Jr. Fund. Earlier, he had been the executive director of Lambda Legal and Gay Men's Health Crisis (GMHC). We've known each other for nearly 40 years as best friends and partners in this work in various ways.

The other person who comes to mind is my first mentor as a young lawyer, Barbara Underwood. She hired me for my first law job out of law school, when she was the appeals bureau chief at the Kings County District Attorney's office. She's now the solicitor general of New York State. She was the first person who really trained me to be a lawyer.

Tim and Barbara were both very committed to training and mentoring. They have different personalities and mentored me in different arenas. Barbara mentored a young lawyer, and Tim mentored an activist. Tim helped sharpen what I would call my leadership skills, some of which I think were innate, and gave me what management skills I acquired. He was probably my most important mentor on that. Each of them valued mentoring, coaching and helping.

Thus far, what have been the worst and best events in your life, and what did those experiences teach you?

One of the best things that ever happened to me was meeting and finally snagging my husband. I, as Marriage, was preaching the freedom to marry, working on the freedom to marry, leading the freedom to marry fight ultimately for over 32 years, most of which time I was single.

I didn't do marriage—or see it as a goal, or articulate it as something crucial—because I personally wanted to get married. That wasn't what was driving me. It was more about history, politics and justice: the right answer, out of fairness and as an engine of change. It wasn't about my own personal wishes.

Once I found somebody willing to put up with me and love me, and then even more so as we built a life together, I found an added reason for the work I do; The power of marriage I had long preached about was something I now experienced and savored. What for me had always been political now was also personal. So having, let's say, the wind beneath my wings, a partner in love, and someone who loves me for me has been the best.

The worst thing that happened to me was an injury that lingered for about a year and a half. It didn't prevent me from functioning in the world, but it was unpleasant and difficult to deal with. It wasn't until it was over and resolved through surgery that I even acknowledged how bad it was. I was unhappy about it, but it was in its own way a testament to my ability to compartmentalize and focus. I realize how lucky I am that even the worst thing that happened to me was something manageable.

What, if anything, keeps you up at night?

I think the same thing that's keeping everybody up all night: How catastrophically awful Trump, the Trump/Pence regime, their Republican enablers in Congress, and the lamentable numbers of people standing by this sinkhole are. It's terrible that the country is on such a wrong track.

What is your definition of happiness, or, what is your philosophy of life?

While I can be curmudgeonly and grumpy, I'm fundamentally a hopeful and optimistic person. I think that's the right way to live life and the right way to get things done. People ask me to share lessons from our victory. They want to know how we did it and what were the elements of success. When I boil it down to three words, I say hope, clarity and tenacity. Relating it to Trump, we're going to need a lot of tenacity.

Our work for every community we care about, for our country as a whole and for a better world, is far from done. We have to keep going and keep fighting; keep our heads up and keep engaging. We will need tenacity.

We don't have full clarity yet, in the way we did with the Freedom to Marry movement, where our clarity of goal and strategy were crucial elements of our success. We don't know the scope of the challenge or the strategy for getting the country back on track, but that clarity will come if we do our work and keep going.

What we need to begin with, though, is hope. We need to have it, and we need to convey it. We have to begin each day, battle and chapter with, "Yes, we can. We can get it back on track. We can change things. This is not the end."

It doesn't help to spend your time wallowing in the negative and cataloging every problem. Yes, things are bad, but don't make a bad thing worse by spending all your time and energy mired in how bad it is. Instead, focus on and convey the pathway and how to move forward. Having that hope, optimism and forward way of thinking is the best way to get progress to happen. It's also the way to rally others to the work, which is essential. And it actually feels better. It gives you the strength to go forward. This is the way I approach life!

What is the greatest misconception about you?

The greatest misconception about me is that I'm really demanding and difficult. I think people think that because I *can* actually be demanding and sometimes difficult—but not as much as they think.

What is the most important thing you tell young people who are thinking about making careers in the nonprofit sector?

Believe you can do it. Believe you can make a difference. Find your passion. Identify your goal and think about what it's going to take to achieve it. Think about your strategy and pathway, and go forward and inspire others to support and train you. You should have the clarity of a goal, believe you can achieve it, and convey that belief. Don't be daunted. Nothing gets done in one day, so stick with it.

In the most important speech I've ever given, "Marriage Equality and the Lessons for the Scary Work of Winning," two of the lessons I put forward were:

Lesson 1: Win trumps loss. You're always going to have losses, but if you achieve your wins, they will enable you to cover your losses.

Lesson 2: Of course, you should aim to win, but when you can't, you should at least fight and engage so that you "lose forward." You can't win every time. You're going to lose. There are going to be losses. Put yourself in a place so that if you continue to work, you will build on your gains even in a losing battle and be in place for the next one. You're not going to achieve or win everything on the opposition's terrain or timeframe, but be clear about where you're going and what you want to achieve. You don't have to know your entire life plan, but know your next goal and where you want to be, and build on that.

If there were one thing you could say to the world's billionaire philanthropists, what would it be?

That investing to scale in a sustained and affirmative campaign to a clear goal and strategy, and in good leadership, pays off, even on a goal that seems unattainable, impractical or impossible to many. Each of those elements is important. Rather than holding on to all your money, it's more rewarding to make the world better and be able to live to see it.

Getting to scale and then winning the Freedom to Marry took time. Gay people had been dreaming of the freedom to marry for decades. It didn't begin with me, or Freedom to Marry, or the period people are familiar with. After the Stonewall rebellion in 1969, gay couples went to courts, seeking the freedom to marry across the country; one of those cases even reached the Supreme Court by 1972.

All those courts rubber-stamped the discrimination; the courts and the country weren't ready. The conversation hadn't happened. I came along in the 1980s and wrote my law school thesis on why gay people should have the freedom to marry and why we should fight for it, proclaiming that we shouldn't take that first no for an answer and that there was a pathway forward.

I believed that fighting for the freedom to marry would be claiming a vocabulary of empathy and shared values that would be an engine of transformation. All of this battling had many ups and downs. In the first 10 years of my working on this, I was cajoling and preaching that we needed to work on this. At that time, most of the movement organizations, the leadership/activist "establishment," were overwhelmed with AIDS and Reagan, and they were divided ideologically and strategically on whether to fight for marriage at all and how. So in that period, it was all about championing, pushing and urging.

Then in the 1990s, we won our first victory with the Hawaii Supreme Court, and that opened up a whole new era.

It was the turning point that launched this ongoing global movement. I was leading this push, mobilizing the work and racking up the battles from a position within one of the key organizations, Lambda Legal.

Lambda did its own fund-raising, and we were trying to get people to support the movement, and trying to build the kind of affirmative sustained campaign that I'd always argued was necessary: which was that we needed to combine public education and political organizing with litigation in order to win. In the '70s, we just had litigation, and it didn't succeed, but in the '90s, we had litigation, and we built some public education and organized politically, but not to scale or with the necessary funding. So we came to the end of the '90s not having won marriage, but having transformed public opinion both among gay and non-gay people.

We saw attacks and mobilization of the opposition. Congress passed this so-called Defense of Marriage Act, states passed these anti-marriage and anti-gay restrictions and legislation. The movement rallied, and people came to believe they could win, even though 20 years earlier they'd been told they couldn't.

The grassroots energy we unleashed by proclaiming the goal and a strategy for winning marriage was huge, but we didn't have significant funding to sustain an affirmative, real campaign. Though we hadn't yet delivered the win, we ended the 1990s with two-thirds of the American people now believing gay people were going to win the freedom to marry, even though we'd begun the decade with people saying it was moronic, ridiculous and impossible. They didn't want us to win the freedom to marry, but they believed we were going to win it.

Then I left Lambda, on friendly terms, in order to build the kind of campaign that I'd been saying was necessary but couldn't be built from just one organization, particularly a legal one. The idea was to create a multi-method, multi-state, multi-partner, multi-year campaign, and thus create a climate that would allow the litigation groups, including Lambda, to succeed. The litigation was still necessary, but it wasn't enough.

I began fund-raising and trying to sell a vision of a campaign that would drive a strategy to a goal and leverage these different organizations and methodologies. I found a seed funder who believed in this vision. They took a leap of faith on a leader and vision and gave what was, at the time, the largest single grant made to the gay movement. And they were giving it not to an organization, but to a guy with an idea. That was the Evelyn & Walter Haas, Jr., Fund, and that's what seeded Freedom to Marry, this new organization that was created as a campaign and wasn't intended to last forever.

We began working to raise money. Haas helped look for others to match them, and they required me to find other funders to come in. What we found was that the vision and the strategy resonated for some, but not at the scale we had urged. So we had to completely revamp the fund-raising plan and shift it to a model that was "If you build it, they will come."

I tried to raise enough money to put in place some of the parts of this campaign, such as the kinds of things we'd be doing, the kind of staff, the central capacity support role, and the strategic voice. That was to galvanize what I still called the "cobble it together" model of getting different organizations to contribute. We played out the 2000s on this model.

Other funders did come in, and in addition to this new organization, Freedom to Marry and the strategy I propounded among key partners (including Lambda Legal and the movement's other legal groups), we created a funder collaborative. This team of funders wasn't yet ready to put all the money into the watering can of Freedom to Marry, but they were willing to water the field according to our strategy, with me as the principal adviser. They came together as the Civil Marriage Collaborative, and I thereby brought an additional couple million dollars annually into the states/building-block element of our strategy and work. It brought us closer, but we were still far from what was needed.

As we gained traction and saw more opportunities to win in courts through legislatures, and ultimately, at the ballot box, we needed to secure more money and also needed political money, not just funds for public education and litigation. Many of these initial funders couldn't do the political work or funding, and the enterprise they were supporting and building wasn't ready to do that. So we were not yet at scale.

By 2010, after years of wrangling, pushing, cajoling and progress, as well as tremendous attacks and blows, it was clear now to many more stakeholders that this "cobble together" model was not to scale and was not what we needed, not only in terms of money but also in terms of focus, infrastructure and political capacity.

Several of those who had resisted my pleading that we needed to take this to a higher level in terms of money, energy, action and commitment now came to me and basically asked me to make it happen. We morphed Freedom to Marry from what was essentially a catalyst to become the actual campaign. I recreated Freedom to Marry as an independent 501(c)(3) and 501(c)(4) nonprofit organization, hired a larger and different staff, going from about 8 people to about 30, as well as a range of consultants and part-time help and advisers.

We had (c)(4) fund-raising as well as (c)(3), and we grew the budget from roughly $600,000 to $13 million. It didn't happen overnight, with one stage, or without many missed opportunities, but by driving our clarity of goal and strategy, we were able to bring people, including funders and donors, along.

We are in the midst of a national conversation about race and racial equity. How did your organization address racial equity?

I am spending a fair amount of time advising and working with other organizations. I'm serving as pro bono senior adviser to the National Immigration Law Center—part of my wanting to respond to the requests for advice and assistance from many organizations and causes eager to hear the lessons and elements of winning, and how other movements can adapt them and build on them.

Obviously, that conversation as regards immigration (and many of the other movements that have come to me) involves race, class and status. With Freedom to Marry, we were very aware of what we were trying to do. We had a three-track strategy: to build a critical mass of state support; build a critical mass of public support; and tackle federal discrimination, in order to create the climate for litigation to succeed nationwide.

In order to build public support, we had to look for the people we could reach. Who were they? What were the shared values that would resonate for them, and what were the stories that would move them? What were the messages that would most engage them, the messengers that would best reach them, the message-delivery venues and drumbeat that would carry the day?

That included looking at people-of-color communities, which obviously overlap with the LGBTQ community (Gay people are black, Latino, Asian, white, etc.). We thought about their needs and vulnerabilities, and who were the people that could help explain those and move them. We delivered programs like *Familia es Familia*, which was intended to raise the visibility and voices of Latino family members (gay and non-gay), in order to make the case for the freedom to marry in those communities, and also to be able to say there was growing Latino support, which mattered in terms of delivering political wins in states with significant Latino populations.

We worked very consciously to enlist leaders and organizations such as the National Association for the Advancement of Colored People (NAACP), Mexican American Legal Defense and Education Fund (MALDEF) and the National Council of La Raza. The very first mainstream organization to endorse Freedom to Marry, other than the American Civil Liberties Union (ACLU), was the Japanese American Citizens League. They did so during the Hawaii chapter, in part, because there was the Hawaii conversation, but also because they were one of the organizations that had litigated *Loving v. Virginia*, and had challenged race restrictions on marriage. They understood the parallels, the language, the arguments and the opponents. We were very conscious of that, and worked those connections and parallels and were respectful of the differences.

We worked to tell the stories of African-American families, Asian families, Latino families. For example, in our program called Let California Ring, designed to build public support in California, we ran ads in eight different languages, including different Asian languages as well as Spanish.

Our opposition worked hard to use race against us. They wanted to pulverize African-American sentiment against gay people by playing the victim card and claiming that we were trying to expropriate civil rights language and the banner of civil rights, and that the gays were displacing people of color. So there were divisions within all communities. There were divisions within all the communities whether it was gay people or people of color, and we had to navigate those dynamics and that divide, even within our own movement and circle.

After the 2016 election, *The New York Times* **reported, "the widening political divergence between cities and small-town America also reflects a growing alienation between the two groups, and a sense—perhaps accurate—that their fates are not connected." What role should the nonprofit sector play in helping the two groups find common ground?**

One of the ways we built support in all parts of the country was by making clear that we are part of every community, and that gay people and people of color are to be found in rural communities. We worked hard to break those stereotypes and raise up diverse messengers to make that case. Our approach was that even rural or red states were part of a national strategy.

Our strategy was to begin where we could win, so even though gay people are found in every state, we have more political power in certain states and urban areas. Although we were aware that we were everywhere and that our job was not done until we had brought along everyone, we bit the bullet and went for wins that would trump losses. We took the inevitable initial losses in many more rural or red states, knowing that we couldn't win everywhere and that we had to win somewhere. So we built where we could build. We had to start where we were strong. As we accumulated our hard-won building blocks, however, we expanded our reach—including investing in a program called Southerners for the Freedom to Marry.

We eventually developed a strategy of working on what we called "progress" states, which were the states where we knew we couldn't win. We didn't need to win there, because our strategy called for building a critical mass of states, and then bringing the country along through a national resolution at the Supreme Court.

We couldn't win the "progress" states, but we could show progress there that would further the national strategy and circle back for the win everywhere. We could show voices, tell stories of families who lived there, show there was more support than people think, show that people were willing to change their minds. It wouldn't be enough to persuade, for example, the Texas Legislature to do the right thing, but enough to show that there was support in Texas, which could then be used in the national effort.

We used calls, voices, events, media; we ran ads, organized campaigns. But that emphasis on the "progress" states, as opposed to building within targeted states, came toward the end. It came where we were trying to solidify the national momentum and the critical mass that would enable us to get the national win that would bring in those other states.

We even used the attacks by our opponents. When George W. Bush called for a constitutional amendment against gay people's freedom to marry, we used that to ratchet up the conversation. We created more buzz and got people talking about it, even in the South. We had more neighbors talking to each other. There were more kids coming out or talking to their parents, and more people started coming out to their roommates, friends and co-workers.

So that's the first point I would make about the rural. We accepted that we couldn't win everywhere on the same timeline. The second point is that even though we couldn't win politically in all those states, we could show progress and momentum, and add that to the national climate creation we were doing. We could underscore that it was unfair that these families were being left out, and therefore, the Supreme Court needed to finish the job and make room for people in those states to do better, to rise to fairness.

By the end, we had won majority support in all four quadrants of the United States, including the South. We had done enough to create a climate that would give the South a voice going forward in the national momentum, and to empower people in the South and in those rural areas to be more open and more supportive.

What is your favorite book?

One of my favorite books is *Memoirs of Hadrian* by Marguerite Yourcenar. It's a beautiful novel, looking back on the life of the Emperor Hadrian, who was essentially gay. He fell in love with a man who died tragically young. Hadrian built statues and cities dedicated to him all across the Roman Empire. It's a reflection on what matters in life and love. I first read it when I was 21, returning from the Peace Corps, and committed to reading it every 10 years, because it's the kind of book that, as you get older, you take different things from it. I also take inspiration from reading Lincoln … and almost any history.

CHAPTER 28

Aria Finger

CEO and Chief Old Person,
DoSomething.org and TMI Strategy

Aria Finger is CEO of DoSomething.org, the largest tech company exclusively for young people and social change, with 5.5 million members in 131 countries. In 2013, she founded TMI Strategy, a subsidiary strategic consultancy that has brought in more than $6 million for DoSomething. Finger graduated with an economics degree from Washington University in St.

Louis, and teaches at New York University. She was named a World Economic Forum Young Global Leader in 2016.

DoSomething.org

DoSomething.org is a global movement for good. It has so far activated 5.5 million young people to make positive change both online and off, in every area code in the United States and in more than 131 countries. It has run major sports-equipment drives, helped to clothe more than half of the teenagers in homeless shelters in the United States, and cleaned up 3.7 million cigarette butts around the world. Its goal is to harness the power and the passion of young people to make a difference on any issue they choose.

Aria Finger

Who has had the greatest influence on you as a professional?

Without question, it would be Nancy Lublin. I arrived at DoSomething in 2005, and she was the CEO at the time. We were a tiny, five-person organization, and I think I was the sixth employee. I worked under Nancy for just over 10 years before I took over about a year and a half ago. She has informed my leadership style and my generosity. She is one of those people who lifts up everyone. I was 25 or 26, and she took me out for a hot chocolate and said, "You're going to be the next CEO of DoSomething. I'm grooming you to be the next CEO." I didn't believe her. I don't even remember if I said no, but I thought no. But she was true to her word. She has given me so much, and the only reason I'm successful today is because of her.

Thus far, what have been the worst and best events in your life, and what did those experiences teach you?

The best thing that ever happened to me is having siblings. It's not that only children can't be wonderful people, but I think the wonderful thing about having siblings is that you can be unabashedly happy for someone else. There is no jealousy. You just want your sibling to succeed so much, so all of their joy is your joy. Conversely, all their pain is your pain.

I'd say the worst thing that ever happened to me was any of my siblings going through tough times, because I just want to help them and lift them up. I want them to be the best, and I can't always affect that change. I think I have a beautiful relationship with my siblings.

What, if anything, keeps you up at night?

I'd say the No. 1 thing that is keeping me up at night right now is the Trump presidency, the political stalemate, and increasing volatility and polarization that is happening in the outside world that also affects young people in America. How can DoSomething be the best organization we can be, to support young people? How can we unite young people so they don't make the same mistakes old people make? The No. 2 thing is giving these young people outlets and a voice. No one cares what 13- to 18-year-olds think, because they can't vote. We pay some lip service to 18- to 25-year-olds, but we don't really care about what they think, but so many of the policy issues directly affect them. We want to make sure we're lifting up these young people's voices and giving them ways to act that aren't polarizing in themselves.

I truly believe that one of the most beautiful things about DoSomething is that we have young people. We have 5.5 million members, and we're diverse in many ways. We're racially diverse; we're in every ZIP code, we have Republicans, Democrats and an increasing number of people who are unaffiliated. I don't want to lose that magical diversity. How do we figure out how to activate young people so they care about these things and avoid increasing the polarization?

What is your definition of happiness, or, what is your philosophy of life?

A lot of people tell me that you shouldn't optimize for happiness, but I'm not one of those people. Happiness and kindness are everything. Of course, if you're optimizing for your own happiness at the expense of the world, that's terrible. I think kindness is incredibly important. My philosophy of life is: How can you maximize happiness for yourself and the world? Then, if you're not happy, do something about it. Not everyone is as lucky as I am, and they may not have the leverage to make change. But if you're one of those privileged folks who actually has the leverage to change it, then stop complaining, and do what you can to change it.

What would you say is the greatest misconception about you?

A lot of people think that I don't have emotion, that I don't cry, or that I don't feel deeply, and that's not true.

What is the most important thing you tell young people who are thinking about making careers in the nonprofit sector?

Do it. The No. 1 thing I tell people is to challenge the premise of the question: What is the nonprofit sector? The ASPCA probably has more in common with Pepsi than the local 10-person nonprofit start-up guys with Warby Parker. Taking the nonprofit sector over here and the for-profit sector over there, and having those be the delineations, doesn't tell you very much about the organization. It tells you almost nothing.

I teach at New York University, and I have students who've had bad experiences interning for nonprofits, so they're turned off by the nonprofit world. I say, "If you had an internship at J.P. Morgan, would you be turned off from the for-profit world?" I wouldn't treat it as a monolith. I'd say it's incredibly diverse, and you can get different experiences. You can be in places that move quickly and places that move slowly. You can be somewhere that's well-paid or somewhere that's not well-paid. I say, figure out what you want to do, then find an organization or company that has that job function, and go from there.

What new opportunities do you see for DoSomething in the next five years?

There are so many. I would say one of the biggest opportunities is doing something about changing a generation of young people. Our campaigns are wonderful, and we make an impact on discrimination, poverty, homelessness and cancer, but our No. 1 goal is changing the young people themselves. We want to make them more confident leaders, more empathetic and lifelong volunteers.

We sort of neglected the political engagement part of that, and after the election, we remembered that the political part of that specific engagement muscle is really important. It means more than just a "Get out and vote" campaign every two or four years. There's so many other things that you need to know about your city council and the importance of going to a school board meeting or calling your state superintendent. I was happy that this election made us think about how we could flex that civil and political engagement muscle. In the next five years, we're going to double down on that.

In the latter half of the next five years, we are going to focus on global expansion. We have members in 131 countries right now. The demand is there, which is really wonderful. In Mexico and Brazil, we have our website in Mexican Spanish and Brazilian Portuguese, with local Mexican content and local Brazilian content. We're seeing the benefits. Conversion rates are going up, and we're seeing more people complete campaigns, so we want to double down on that global perspective.

I think there's an even greater opportunity for TMI, an earned income consultancy that is part of DoSomething. We help brands understand Gen Z and millennials as it relates to social change. As more nonprofits get older, they're going to be doubling down even more on young people. A lot of these legacy organizations are really going to struggle without understanding the younger generation, so there's a huge opportunity for us to help them. I also think the brands will continue to tiptoe around social change, but they won't abandon it. They're going to continue to understand that young people are demanding social change from their brands, and we want to help them get it right. Bad marketing hurts everyone, and bad social change campaigns hurt everyone. There's enormous potential to grow TMI, do more good for the world, and bring more revenue into the company.

We are in the midst of a national conversation about race and racial equity. What is your organization doing, both internally and externally, to address racial inequity?

Internally, we really pride ourselves on being a racially diverse workforce. You can see in the numbers that we over-indexed the national average for people of color who work here, but there's more to it than just numbers. A few years ago, we implemented an anonymous biannual happiness survey just to gauge how everyone is feeling about every-thing from their manager, to what we're doing, to transpar-ency. Several of the questions we ask are about racial equity within the organization, and how they feel we're addressing diversity from all sides.

One of the questions that came out loud and clear from that survey was why we weren't doing diversity training in the office. It was clear that staffers wanted to do diversity training. We hired a wonderful moderator and took a day in diversity and communication training. It was really wonder-ful. We had lessons on micro-aggressions, how to commu-nicate and assuming positive intent. Now, when we look at our happiness survey, we've seen increases in folks for hap-piness, with both the level of diversity on staff and how they think we're dealing with it.

From an external perspective, many of our campaigns deal with the issue of racial inequity. Some deal with this issue head on. We just wrapped a campaign called "Suspended for What?" This has to do with black and Latino kids being sus-pended at four times the rate of white kids for similar infrac-tions. I'm very passionate about criminal justice reform, and I never thought that criminal justice reform and DoSomething could come together, but it makes perfect sense. Kids get suspended, then expelled, and when they get picked up for graffiti, the white kid who has no suspension gets a slap on the wrist, and the black kid who does have a suspension goes to Juvenile Hall. It really is the start of the trajectory. We're running several campaigns that explicitly take on racial prejudice and discrimination.

We're also looking at racial inequity within our other campaigns. We just launched a campaign with Johnson & Johnson called "Give a Spit About Cancer." It's all about getting more young people on the bone marrow registry. If you have leukemia or blood cancer, you need a bone marrow transplant. Seventy percent of folks get a transplant outside their family. College students have the best bone marrow because 18- to 24-year-olds have the best bone marrow. There aren't enough people on the list, so we ran this campaign, and it's saving lives.

But if you look into the numbers, you'll see that if you're white, the chance of finding a match is over 90 percent. If you're a person of color, the chance of finding a match is under 70 percent. That is a massive disparity, just based on race. So we thought of running this campaign to get more nonwhite people on the bone marrow registry. We targeted historically black colleges; we just used their own racially diverse lists. Looking at a campaign like that through the lens of race is wonderful, because we can really move the needle in ways that the organization might not be able to.

A 2016 U.S. Trust study shows that high net worth Americans have greater confidence in individuals and

nonprofits than in the executive branch or Congress. With the current administration and Congress, what role should the nonprofit sector and organizations like yours play over the next several years?

We were created to pick up the slack that was left behind between the government and the for-profit world. We're supposed to be for the underdog and make sure we're protecting the rights of targeted minorities. We're supposed to be standing up for the folks who don't have power or a voice, whether it's an economic voice for low-income Americans or protecting Muslim Americans. There's been increased hatred in these times.

I think we have an obligation to look at our campaigns and make sure we're looking at racial inequities. We're running a campaign right now called "Sincerely Us" which involves sending teen-made "Happy Ramadan" cards to every single mosque in America. It sends the message that the teens of America have your back and are fighting for freedom of religion, and supporting all people. Those are some of the folks that are being targeted right now, so we should step up and make sure they are not afraid.

After the 2016 election, *The New York Times* reported, "the widening political divergence between cities and small-town America also reflects a growing alienation between the two groups, and a sense—perhaps accurate—that their fates are not connected." What role should the nonprofit sector play in helping the two groups find common ground?

I think the divide between cities and rural communities is incredibly important. Of course, their fates are intertwined.

The future of America is intertwined in folks believing that we should exist—just like the whole stock market is based on whether we believe in it. It's critically important for the nonprofit sector to look at this, and that doesn't mean prioritizing this sort of mythical white, low-income voter.

There's been too much talk about separating folks into camps, with city-minded racially diverse people over here and low-income white rural people over there. I don't think going to the rural areas and talking to people is the thing to do. We need to realize that our fates are intertwined and lift everyone up. I think it's unfortunate that, for some reason, the words "working-class" now mean "white." If we're going to help low-income Americans, that means helping more women than men and more minorities than white people. There are so many groups that are encompassed in this group of low-income Americans, so we need to make sure we help them out, and we'll also help a lot of these other targeted minorities.

What is one thing you would tell your colleagues who are leading grant-making foundations?

That's easy: "Go out and DoSomething." I would say to talk to people who don't have to be nice to you because you're funding them or because they want you to fund them. I think that's the biggest problem. One of the challenges of a CEO of a company or foundation is that everyone wants your money. Everyone wants your approval, so people tell you what you want to hear, and that's a really tough thing to break.

Could you give some advice to your colleagues in the nonprofit sector about how to diversify the staff?

First of all, I'd say that I don't have all of the answers. Our staff and board are very diverse in general, but if you look at our C-suite, it's not as diverse as we'd like it to be in terms of racial diversity. All I can say is that we're aware of our shortcomings and we're always trying to work on them!

A few things that we have done and/or learned from that might be helpful: Of course, racially diverse places attract racially diverse people. It's hard to hire a black woman if you have no women and no black people in your company, and I understand that. I often hear that people feel that they can hire diverse staff, but they can't retain them. I'm hoping that people realize that perhaps more than half the battle is thinking about retention. That's why we try to focus on feedback from employees, both anonymous and direct. It's perhaps harder to do at bigger companies and at companies where you're afraid of liability, but I find our feedback mechanisms incredibly valuable, whether that's our bi-annual anonymous survey, our "Ask me anything" C-level dinners, skip-level reviews, etc.

I would just be as honest and transparent as possible as to where you're falling short. People don't expect you to be perfect, but they do expect you to tell the truth. Another piece of advice I would give, especially when you're talking about a diverse class of young people, is to think about intersectionality. I'm a woman, so I'm "diverse" in one way, but I'm also straight, cisgender and white. I can try to understand the experiences of others who are more diverse, but I can't understand everything, because I didn't live that experience.

So really looking at intersectionality of diversity is important. If you're only prioritizing people who are one level adjacent from the "typical" straight white man who gets a pass more easily into this world, then you may need to look deeper.

Another thing we do is track our college interns in terms of the education level of their parents, income level, racial diversity, gender diversity, sexual orientation and where they're from. About a quarter of our staff is made of former interns, so there's a great hiring pipeline for us, and we start tracking it there so we can ensure diversity.

CHAPTER 29

Take Action

In the course of interviewing for and writing this book, we have been astounded by what we learned from our interviewees about nonprofit leadership and management. We have found their wisdom deeply inspiring, motivating and, ultimately, practical. This chapter distills some of our favorite insights into action steps that can greatly benefit you, your organization, and your community.

Sharpen Your Leadership Skills

Always remember where you came from. Your roots make you strong—and uniquely qualified to deal with life's challenges.

Seek joy—not happiness—through serving others, in your work and your life. Be hopeful—not optimistic—in your outlook. Katharine Henderson of Auburn Seminary says it best.

"I don't resonate with the word happiness at all. Happiness, like optimism, is a light word. I think they are words that are too sought after by our culture. I don't think that you become happy in life by seeking happiness. And I think people are often thrown completely off course in their lives because they're trying to seek after something called happiness. And the more you seek after it, the more it will elude you. So joy is deeper than happiness. Hope is deeper than optimism. And for me, both are connected to something beyond oneself. I would call it faith; other people would call it other things."

When we asked Naomi Levine of New York University what her philosophy of life was, she summed it up succinctly: love, friendship and meaningful work.

Even when you have achieved success, remain committed to learning and becoming a better leader. It is easy to become complacent, as Henry Timms of 92Y noted.

Educate yourself further about the origins of and solutions to racial and economic inequity. No one can call him/herself a leader today without understanding what has led to so much needless suffering. Equally important is learning about what works in moving past the pain to real solutions.

Bob Giannino of uAspire has a particularly poignant take on the discrepancy between uAspire's mission and the composition of its staff. He comes from a white, working-class neighborhood in Boston and was the first in his family to have gone to college. His parents were high school dropouts.

His staff is quite diverse, but at the top it is mostly white. He says, "Somewhere along the way, I lost sight of where I came from. The organization I lead is overall very diverse, but at the leadership level, it's very white."

Bob's story underscores for us the difficulty of seeing the racial equity issue clearly. After all, Bob comes from a background that is not dissimilar to that of the organization's clients. Yet even he, after attending an elite college and having his life's direction changed forever by it, struggles to stay connected to his roots.

Even the most compassionate leaders, as they build institutions, sometimes lose relationships. Do not be afraid of this. Katharine Henderson expresses it this way. "I'm aware that there are people along the way whom I have let down and from whom I have become estranged—people who have worked with me and for me, relationships that didn't work institutionally or personally. It's one of the hazards of running an institution. It's inevitable in one's personal life and as the head of an institution."

Remember to take the work, but not yourself, seriously. So many of you are working on life-and-death issues all the time. Without humor, it is very difficult to keep going for the long term.

Be a contrarian. Follow your intuition. Think differently from others around you and from other institutions. Reinvent the way you do things, rather than follow the herd.

This is advice often given, but not so easily followed. It is also somewhat controversial, because many in the mainstream believe creativity is enhanced, not diminished, by interactions with others. We say go into your cave to invent, then come out to talk to people, refine and improve your invention.

Ensure Your Own House Is in Order

Be clear about whether your organization is about changing society or helping others. Both have merit, but they call for different skill sets and personalities.

As long as the goal of a project is clear, let those who work with and for you find their own ways to that goal.

Make sure to celebrate the small wins as well as the big ones.

This advice from Brian Gallagher, CEO of United Way Worldwide, really stayed with us. Do you have an employee who successfully completed a difficult project? Did someone on your staff figure out a better way to route packages from the mailroom? Did someone at your office successfully complete a marathon, or even a half-marathon? All these could be reasons to acknowledge the employee and let the team know you are paying attention to what they do well, not just what goes wrong.

Consider integrating your major donors, slowly, into organizational decision-making.

The days when donors just wrote big checks and read annual reports are over. Those with new wealth, in particular, want to be involved in deciding how their dollars are spent and how results are measured. This means educating donors about your programs, the environment in which your organization operates and other organizations operating in your space. It also means informing them about how your organization is similar to a corporation and how it is different.

Hire fund-raisers, particularly major gift fund-raisers, who are intelligent, like to read and can carry on good conversations.

Naomi Levine, for many years the vice president of development at New York University, says, "If you are an interesting, intelligent human being, you can do well in fund-raising. If you don't read, and you're not able to sustain intelligent conversation in a relationship, you never will do well." If you are going to be cultivating as your major donors people of influence and affluence, they will relate best to fund-raisers who can ask about what they have been reading and carry on an intelligent conversation about it. Everything else can be learned.

This has been our experience. We recently hired a young woman with virtually no fund-raising experience who is extremely bright, has an MFA and is passionate about the mission of our client. She did so well in the first three months of the assignment that we recommended that the client hire her for a responsible fund-raising job, despite her lack of experience. She is already a great asset to the organization.

Once you decide to diversify your Board, be single-minded about it. Don't be afraid to say no to qualified candidates who don't meet your diversity criteria. And remember you can always find people of means who meet your diversity criteria.

Think more about re-recruiting people than about communicating with them.

This excellent advice comes from Tom Dente of Humentum. He makes the point that there is a lot of talk about improving communication, both inside the organization and with its external stakeholders. Some of that really needs to happen. But more often than not, if people feel connected to the organization, its mission, values and vision, they will be more satisfied and not need communication just for the sake of saying you put out your monthly employee newsletter. In other words, you must engage your employees from the moment they walk through your doors.

Be Crystal Clear About Your Goal; Articulate It Persuasively

Set ambitious goals for yourself, even when those goals seem almost impossible to achieve.

An example of such goal setting is the making of this book. We had never produced a book before, and the project seemed absurdly overwhelming. But we decided to go ahead anyway. We missed our first self-imposed deadlines for finishing the interviews, and kept going—with a minimum of self-criticism. We didn't know how to find a printer, but we kept asking people and eventually identified the best one for us. We had never created a marketing plan for a book but created one anyway, with help from our business coach.

Even if you are not good at the "vision thing," get good enough to inspire the people you work with. Having a clear vision for your organization and its contribution to making a better world is critical in persuading other people to work hard toward that world.

As Shael Polakow-Suransky of Bank Street College says, "People will work really hard and go far out of their way if they feel they could have an impact."

In our experience, most boards of directors look to their CEOs to generate a vision for the organization, share it with them and work with them to refine it.

The vision consists of a bold, stretch goal and a vivid description of what will be different either within the company or outside when the vision is achieved. Working with your staff and board to identify that big goal and the description that accompanies it can be a thrilling process, not the usual boring exercise so many of us associate with crafting mission and vision statements. We have done it successfully many times with clients.

"Lean in with the audacity of ambition," says Nonet Sykes of the Annie E. Casey Foundation.

Using your position to the fullest, not shying away from the power you have, is key both to advancing professionally and to making the world a better place. This is a good piece of advice for men and women. Often, young people think they cannot express their opinions or beliefs because others will not listen to or take them seriously. If you end up in an organization where you are not able to express yourself, please find another job. The world has many social problems, and all of us are needed to solve them. Age is not a prerequisite for wisdom.

Beware the quantitative results trap, but get serious about measuring impact.

Many of the methodologies that are now being used to measure nonprofit impact were developed for health care. Think of the randomized control trial, developed to measure the effectiveness of one treatment over another. Some of the methodologies used to measure success in educational achievement were developed with that model in mind. There are lots of well-publicized issues with this approach.

Suransky thinks the approach taken by the technology sector, sometimes known as "lean start-up," is a better way to measure the effectiveness of certain social programs. In lean start-up, you create a prototype of the product and test it, then go back and change it, based on feedback. You do this many times before you arrive at the product you will bring to market.

Darlene Fedun, CEO of Bethel Woods Center for the Arts, calls it piloting: "A good deal of our success has come from piloting programs, and developing projects and pro-grams that are scalable and/or have the ability to be done in phases. It's a way to test, prove, present and gain larg-er-scale support. This is especially important in rural regions that have limited resources and accessibility."

Campaign on Many Fronts

The theme of nonprofits acting as a means to find com-mon ground arose numerous times during our interviews. Several of our interviewees used gun control as an example.

Naomi Levine says, "We have to act as a bridge. I have friends in suburban Connecticut, and I have reached out to them on the issues. What do both of us have in common?

We're shocked at the number of guns in America, and so are they. And so they have joined various groups with us to fight for better gun control. I think that nonprofits connect as bridges, giving their hands to those in the suburban areas around issues that we agree upon."

In addition to changing social norms, nonprofits must recognize when norms have changed and act accordingly. Henry Timms at 92Y is highly attuned to this need. He says, "The issue that organizations get into is so many of them are built on old power norms, which is, 'We've got all the power, we're very prestigious, we're very influential, people listen to us, we're going to send you our annual report and expect you to read it.' That set of skills and behaviors is actually very different from the one which the new generation needs, which is: They need leaders who are going to prepare to give up power rather than hold on to it."

Build Broad-Based Coalitions

Focus on gaining the means to build partnerships. Karen Meyerhoff is president and executive director of Wave Hill, a 28-acre public garden and cultural center in the Bronx overlooking the Hudson River and the Palisades. She has had tremendous experience with partnerships. Before she worked at Wave Hill, she spent 10 years at the Museum of Modern Art and also worked at the Metropolitan Museum of Art and the Guggenheim Museum. She says, "People do business with people they like. They are loyal in those partnerships, sometimes more than they are for the business rewards." Remember that partnerships often have contracts attached to them, but the real glue in the partnership is the relationships formed between the representatives of the deliberating organizations.

We are fascinated by the possibility of considering faith-based communities as indispensable partners in making change.

Katharine Henderson of Auburn says, "We have a lot of conversations with foundations to help them think about their power. I would say not to underestimate the power and importance of faith in social change. People often see religion as a problem, but religion and faith-rooted folks are often part of the solution. Faith gives you a framework for justice that's deeply rooted in tradition and language. It helps to sustain people when the going gets really tough."

Leon Botstein of Bard College agrees: "One of the things we try to do at Bard is improve the conversation by providing services, opening lines of communication, and working collaboratively with constituencies and communities with which we may actually disagree. For a long time, to our peril, we ignored communities of faith, believing somehow that religion was a dying phenomenon. We have to communicate with people who legitimately find comfort in faith and in communities of faith."

Persist

Most people—not all—need work-life balance in their lives to do their best work and feel satisfied with it.

Karen Meyerhoff of Wave Hill says, "I think it is important to have balance, particularly for young mothers. Don't ask permission. If you have a child care issue, go take care of it. Tell me you are not going to be here, so I don't go looking for you, but just go take care of it. Stuff comes up when you have kids at home. There has to be balance. It is not healthy otherwise."

We love this approach and wish more employers would adopt it.

Learn from those who never give up.

Dan Gross says, "One of the things that stuck out when I met Sarah Brady [co-founder of the Brady Campaign to Prevent Gun Violence] was her dogged determination and strength. She faced every day with such optimism. Prior to my brother being shot, I don't think I was capable of that. I didn't see myself single-mindedly focusing on something, but now I know I can do it."

Leverage Your Success

Invest in tomorrow's leaders.

Nonprofits must do their part in educating the American workforce. Think about creating or expanding your internship program. Include high school and college students in the areas where you have offices.

Have a succession plan.

As Paula Kerger of PBS put it, have a No. 2 even if you know that person is not the one to succeed you. That way, if the worst happens, someone has the authority to pilot the ship while the board searches for a new CEO.

Final Thoughts

Leaders will always fascinate us. We can learn so much from them.

We wrote this book for several reasons. We perceived a lack of public awareness of the profound, life-affirming changes effected by today's nonprofit leaders. Our goal was to amplify the leading voices of the nonprofit sector, because the good news about their successful strategies and impact is rarely recorded or reported.

While books abound on the topic of for-profit leadership, few books are devoted to nonprofit leadership. We wanted to combine our experience working in the sector with what we learned from the interviews, to help other professionals and philanthropists improve their own organizations' impact.

Our questions elicited inspiring stories about triumphs and tragedies, about gain and loss. We also heard about the practical aspects of sparking social change. Great leaders call forth the best in us because they balance head and heart, intellect and soul.

Like the leaders we interviewed, all of us in the nonprofit sector are driven by a deep desire to contribute toward creating a better life now and in the future. And we know instinctively that we can achieve far more together than any of us could accomplish alone.

APPENDIX 1

Complete List of Interviewees

1. Blackwell, Fred, CEO, San Francisco Foundation
2. Botstein, Leon, President, Bard College
3. Calvin, Kathy, President & CEO, United Nations Foundation
4. Capasso, Michael, General Director, New York City Opera
5. Cardinali, Dan, President & CEO, Independent Sector
6. Chaudhry, Muhammed, President & CEO, Silicon Valley Education Foundation
7. Cooks, Gali, Executive Director, Leading Edge
8. Dente, Thomas, President & CEO, Humentum
9. Edelsberg, Chip, former CEO, Jim Joseph Foundation
10. Fedun, Darlene, CEO, Bethel Woods Center for the Arts
11. Finger, Aria, CEO & Chief Old Person, DoSomething. org and TMI Strategy

12. Forrester, Robert, President & CEO, Newman's Own Foundation

13. Gallagher, Brian, President & CEO, United Way Worldwide

14. Giannino, Bob, CEO, uAspire

15. Gibbons, James, President & CEO, Goodwill Industries International

16. Gross, Dan, President, Brady Campaign to Prevent Gun Violence

17. Heintz, Stephen, President, Rockefeller Brothers Fund

18. Henderson, Katharine, President, Auburn Seminary

19. Hockenbury, Alice, VP Public Policy and Advocacy, Girl Scouts of America

20. Houston, Amy, Managing Director for Management Assistance and Administration, Robin Hood Foundation

21. Kerger, Paula, President & CEO, PBS

22. Kramer, Larry, President, William and Flora Hewlett Foundation

23. LaPointe, Ellen, President & CEO, Northern California Grantmakers

24. Levine, Naomi, Special Adviser to the Dean, NYU School of Professional Studies

25. McClimon, Tim, President, American Express Foundation

26. McLaren, Brian, Co-founder, Convergence Network

27. McMahon, J. Kevin, CEO, Pittsburgh Cultural Trust

28. Meyerhoff, Karen, President & Executive Director, Wave Hill

29. O'Connell, Jane, CEO, B. Altman Foundation

30. Osberg, Sally, CEO, Skoll Foundation

31. Palmer, Stacy, Editor, *The Chronicle of Philanthropy*

32. Pennington, Hilary, Vice President, Education, Creativity and Free Expression, Ford Foundation

33. Perry, Tara, CEO, National CASA

34. Polakow-Suransky, Shael, President, Bank Street College

35. Shapiro, Neal, President, Channel 13 WNET

36. Shore, Bill, Founder & CEO, Share Our Strength

37. Siegal, James, CEO, KaBOOM! Inc.

38. Stoneman, Dorothy, Founder & CEO, YouthBuild USA

39. Sykes, Nonet, Director of Racial and Ethnic Equity and Inclusion, Annie E. Casey Foundation

40. Syms, Marcy, President, Sy Syms Foundation

41. Timms, Henry, Executive Director, 92Y

42. Ulfelder, Bill, NY Executive Director, Nature Conservancy

43. Walker, Laura, President & CEO, New York Public Radio

44. Washington, Kevin, President & CEO, YMCA of the USA

45. Williams, Kimberly, CEO, Mental Health Association of New York City

46. Wolfson, Evan, Founder & President, Freedom to Marry

47. Younger, Teresa C., President & CEO, Ms. Foundation for Women

APPENDIX 2

Recommended Reading

Leadership

For great advice on goal-setting, please refer to *The Magic Lamp: Goal Setting for People Who Hate Setting Goals*,[18] and a perennial favorite, *The 7 Habits of Highly Effective People*,[19] first published almost three decades ago and still in print.

Our favorite article—ever—on vision is "Building Your Company's Vision," by Jim Collins and Jerry Porras.[20] Collins and Porras argue that great organizations have a rare ability to grow and change while staying true to their core purpose. The organization's vision helps to define the strategies and

---

18   Keith Ellis: *The Magic Lamp: Goal Setting for People Who Hate Setting Goals* (New York: Three Rivers Press, 1998).
19   Stephen R. Covey: *The 7 Habits of Highly Effective People* (New York: Simon & Schuster, 1989).
20   Jim Collins and Jerry I. Porras: "Building Your Company's Vision" (Boston: *Harvard Business Review*, September 1996).

tactics that should change, while providing guidance on what should stay the same.

Here are two books to read if you feel you have reached a plateau in your leadership and want to go to the next level. The first is *Extreme Ownership: How U.S. Navy SEALs Lead and Win*, written by two Navy SEALs who served together in Iraq.[21] This may seem an odd suggestion from two writers committed to creating a more enlightened world. But it is often acknowledged that military leadership training is a gold standard.

The second is *Superbosses: How Exceptional Leaders Master the Flow of Talent*, by Sydney Finkelstein.[22] Finkelstein did over 200 interviews for the book over 10 years, and identified three main characteristics of those who are consistently rated the highest by their employees. They create master-apprentice relationships, rely on the cohort effort and say good-bye on good terms, as talented employees leave for better jobs.

We especially recommend a couple of books for women aspiring to leadership roles. The first is *The Next Generation of Women Leaders: What You Need to Lead but Won't Learn in Business School*.[23] Written by Selena Rezvani, this book is aimed at young women like herself whose goal is reaching the top echelons of any organization.

---

21 Jocko Willink and Leif Babin: *Extreme Ownership: How U.S. Navy SEALs Lead and Win* (New York: St. Martin's Press, 2015).
22 Sydney Finkelstein: *Superbosses: How Exceptional Leaders Master the Flow of Talent*. (Portfolio/Penguin, 2016).
23 Selena Rezvani: *The Next Generation of Women Leaders: What You Need to Lead but Won't Learn in Business School* (California: Praeger, 2010).

Also be sure to read *Nice Girls Don't Get the Corner Office: 101 Unconscious Mistakes Women Make That Sabotage Their Careers* by Lois Frankel, PhD. She has written a number of excellent books on the psychological stumbling blocks that women encounter as they become leaders.[24]

Here is a book that offers straightforward career advice to women at all levels. It is *I Shouldn't Be Telling You This: Success Secrets Every Gutsy Girl Should Know*, by Kate White.[25]

And for those moments when you have the workplace blues, a humor-tinged blog called *Nonprofit: Awesomely Fabulous*[26] can lift your spirits. Its motto is "Exploring the fun and frustrations of nonprofit work."

Management

Our favorite book on nonprofit management is *The Progress Principle*, by Teresa Amabile and Steven Kramer.[27] Amabile and Kramer conducted extensive research to discover how managers can foster progress and enhance the inner work life of their employees on a daily basis. They discovered that making meaningful progress on meaningful work is the No. 1 determinant of employee satisfaction. They also explain how to activate two forces that enable progress:

24   Lois Frankel, PhD: *Nice Girls Don't Get the Corner Office: 101 Unconscious Mistakes Women Make That Sabotage Their Careers* (New York: Warner Business Books, 2004).

25   Kate White, *I Shouldn't Be Telling You This* (New York, HarperBusiness, 2012).

26   See http://nonprofitaf.com/.

27   Teresa Amabile and Steven Kramer, *The Progress Principle: Using Small Wins to Ignite Joy, Engagement and Creativity at Work* (Boston: Harvard Business Review Press, 2011).

catalysts—events that directly facilitate project work, and nourishers—interpersonal events that uplift workers.

A good monograph on measuring the impact of your nonprofit's programs is *Leap of Reason: Managing to Outcomes in an Era of Scarcity*, by philanthropist Mario Marino.[28] He argues that, in today's world, nonprofits are going to have to get much better at demonstrating impact when they seek funding and other resources from donors.

In lean start-ups, you create a prototype of the product and test it, then go back and change it based on feedback. The book *The Lean Startup: How Today's Entrepreneurs Use Continuous Innovation to Create Radically Successful Businesses*, by Eric Ries,[29] is on its way to becoming a classic in this area.

Also highly recommended by a friend who runs an incubator for students at a university is *Business Model Generation: A Handbook for Visionaries, Game Changers and Challengers* by Alexander Osterwalder and Yves Pigneur.[30]

Blue Avocado, a magazine of American nonprofits, published a three-part series on board diversity in nonprofits in 2012. The first installment was called "A Fresh Look at

---

28   *Mario Marino: Leap of Reason: Managing to Outcomes in an Era of Scarcity.* (Washington, DC: Venture Philanthropy Partners, 2011).

29   Eric Ries: *The Lean Startup: How Today's Entrepreneurs Use Continuous Innovation to Create Radically Successful Businesses.* (New York: Crown Business, 2011).

30   Alexander Osterwalder and Yves Pigneur: *Business Model Generation: A Handbook for Visionaries, Game Changers and Challengers* (New York: John Wiley & Sons, Inc., 2010).

Diversity and Boards."[31] It gives four reasons for diversity: mission, business, definitional and responsible corporation.

For further evidence that diversity is becoming a prerequisite for a high-performing board, read an article called "Corporate Board Diversity Gets Push from Business Leaders" from late 2016.[32]

For insights on following your individual intuition rather than the herd mentality, read *Fostering Creativity*, a blog by Ken Eisold, PhD, for *Psychology Today*.[33]

One of our interviewees, Jim Gibbons of Goodwill Industries, thinks highly of Jamie Merisotis, president of the Lumina Foundation, one of the largest foundations in the United States and a driving force for increasing Americans' success in higher education. We recommend Merisotis' book, *America Needs Talent: Attracting, Educating & Deploying the 21st Century Workforce*.[34] It lays out his prescription for growing talent in the United States, from rethinking higher education to transforming immigration laws, revitalizing urban hubs and encouraging private sector innovation.

Much has been written in the past several years about employee engagement. Here are the first of a few books we

---

31   Jan Masaoka, "A Fresh Look at Diversity and Boards," (*Blue Avocado*, 2012), http://www.blueavocado.org/content/fresh-look-diversity-and-boards.

32   Michael W. Peregrine, "Corporate Board Diversity Gets Push from Business Leaders" (*The New York Times*, Oct. 12, 2016). https://www.nytimes.com/2016/10/14/business/dealbook/corporate-board-diversi-ty-gets-push-from-business-leaders.html?_r=0.

33   Ken Eisold, PhD, "Fostering Creativity" (*Psychology Today*, Feb. 18, 2012). https://www.psychologytoday.com/blog/hidden-motives/201202/fostering-creativity.

34   Jamie Merisotis, *America Needs Talent: Attracting, Educating & Deploying the 21st Century* Workforce (New York: Rosetta Books, 2015

recommend: *Activate Leadership: Aspen Truths to Inspire Millennial Leadership* by Jon Mertz.[35] Mertz makes the case that millennials, like aspen trees, are "connection-rich, purpose-filled and community-centered".[36]This quality is a great foundation for leadership in a world where team efforts and collaboration are more essential than ever.

Last but not least is *Getting to the Heart of Employee Engagement: The Power and Purpose of Imagination and Free Will in the Workplace* by Les Landes.[37] In this office fable, a young human resources manager spends a few magical days with a mysterious consultant who coaches him on performance management, continuous improvement and communication. It is a unique, engaging format that will pique any reader's interest.

35   Jon Mertz: *Activate Leadership: Aspen Truths to Empower Millennial Leaders.* (Thin Difference, 2015).
36   Ibid, p. 12.
37   Les Landes, *Getting to the Heart of Employee Engagement: The Power and Purpose of Imagination and Free Will in the Workplace* (iUniverse, 2012).

ACKNOWLEDGMENTS

It definitely takes a village to write and publish a book.

We are grateful to our many clients over the years. They have taught us much about the art and science of leadership.

We thank all 50 leaders we interviewed. They were generous with their time, their insights and their wisdom.

Our business coach, Chris Cayer, gave us invaluable counsel every step of the way, from the book's conception to its final delivery.

Our marketing friend Leslie Zane asked us brilliant questions that led us to the overarching theme of the book.

Our executive assistant, Andrew Franco, tirelessly transcribed and edited interviews and helped us create the book's cover.

Our cover designer, Armend Meha, produced a great cover in record time.

The H2Growth team, friends and family members advised us on the best book title.

Our copy editor, Vicky Elliott, went above and beyond the call of duty to ensure proper use of the English language.

We had a proofreading posse of 10 friends and family who, over one weekend, read and commented on the entire manuscript.

And our friend Amelia Weiss read the book one last time before it went to print.

ABOUT THE AUTHORS

VIVIEN HOEXTER, a principal of H2Growth Strategies LLC, advises nonprofits and foundations on developing high-impact strategies, marketing more effectively, and increasing contributed and earned revenues. She coaches executives in leadership roles and/or transitioning to new ones. She holds an MBA from the Wharton School of the University of Pennsylvania.

LINDA C. HARTLEY, a principal of H2Growth Strategies LLC, offers an integrated approach to planning and development that is informed by an MBA in management from NYU and more than 30 years experience in meeting fundraising goals, working with and training volunteer leadership, directing capital campaigns, and managing development and communications programs for both large and small nonprofit organizations.

ABOUT H2GROWTH STRATEGIES LLC

H2Growth Strategies provides counsel on planning, development and governance to mission-driven organizations— nonprofits, foundations and corporations—for improved performance, increased revenues and lasting social impact for a more enlightened world. With its team of specialists, the organization has helped 100 nonprofits raise more than $1.5 billion.